Dear Chris,

    It's a great profession. Enjoy, Enjoy — Sure, sometimes it's not a bed of roses, but those ~~Fatines~~ will make us ~~strngth~~ stretch. May our paths cross again —

Ruth app

Nov. '03

The author has provided a history of struggles, obstacles, disappointments and outstanding achievements of females who determined to and have taken their rightful place as officers of the Court in our justice system. This book is a tribute to them and should be of great interest to lawyers and the public in general.

—LeRoy and Marian Nettles
Father and daughter attorneys of Lake City

Having been admitted to the bar in 1952, and having been continuously practicing law both as trial attorney and in general practice since that time, I can attest to the transition from an almost all male profession to a profession which has female lawyers performing successfully in trials, Estate Planning, Real Estate and all other phases of the practice of law, and also serving as Judges, both on the trial level and in the Appellate Courts.

Ruth Cupp's book brings out the detail of this transition and adds color as well to make it interesting reading both to lawyers and laymen.

—Hall Yarborough
Orangeburg attorney

The artist prophetically sculpted a woman holding the Scales of Justice, now more equally balanced, thanks to decades of action by women who dared to be lawyers. Ruth W. Cupp has set South Carolina women lawyers like jewels in a grand historic perspective in this compelling, inspirational book.

—Leo H. and Dr. Grace Hill
Greenville Attorney and wife

Portia Steps Up to the Bar

The First Women Lawyers of South Carolina

Portia Steps Up to the Bar

The First Women Lawyers of South Carolina

Ruth Williams Cupp

Ivy House
Publishing Group

www.ivyhousebooks.com

PUBLISHED BY IVY HOUSE PUBLISHING GROUP
5122 Bur Oak Circle, Raleigh, NC 27612
United States of America
919-782-0281
www.ivyhousebooks.com

ISBN: 1-57197-369-9
Library of Congress Control Number: 2003101587

Printed in the United States of America

To all Pioneer Portias

To Jean Baker Carson and
Dr. John Hammond Moore

Table of Contents

Acknowledgments

This book is a collaboration between the writer, the editor, the research associates and the readers.

To those essential, life-sharing loved ones who contributed to this project: Claude M. "Bud" Cupp, Jean Vance Bowles, Jean Baker Carson, J. Lawrence Duffy, Eddie Lou Garvin, Nancy Gebhardt, Claire and Ben Goldberg, Mary Green, Patsy W. Hughes, Dr. Robert Marks, Dr. John Hammond Moore, Louise Pettus, Dr. Ruth Roettinger, Milton D. Stratos, Sarah Watson, Sonja Weston, Barbara S. Williams, Betty Jean Wood, M.D.

In addition to the lawyers whose names are mentioned in the book, there were many others who helped: Samuel H. Altman, Russell Brown, Judge Carol Conner, John K. DeLoach, Robert McC.Figg, Cindy M. Floyd, Charles S. Goldberg, Blenzy Gore, Edward A. Harter, Jr., W. Brantley Harvey, Jr., U.S. Senator Earnest F. Hollings and staff, Dan E. Laney, Wade H. Logan, III, Morris D. Mazursky, Judge Amy W. McCulloch, G. Sims McDowell, III, Judge Joseph H. Mendelshon, Venus Nipper, William M. O'Bryan, Judge Matthew Perry, Jr., William A. Ruth, Edward E. Saleeby, Sr., A. Bernard Solomon, J. D. Todd, Judge John H. Waller.

To those family members who have a special interest in this history, as they are related to early women lawyers, thank you for your assistance: Walton Carlisle Beeson, Leola Kearsey Benjamin, Bessie Boykin, Jeanne Briggs, Mary W. Carson, Caroline Ellerbe, Lynn Scarborough Evans, H. B. Free, Neda Gibbons, Elsie Taylor Goins, Eleanor Allan Hanson, Mary Heider, Edwina S. Kennedy, Milton Marcus, Bettie Lee Huggins McAlister, Margie McCay, Elsie H. Taylor Owens, Nancy Prosser, Mary Jo Ross, Col. James A. Sloan,

D. Lesesne Smith, III, Mary Helen Spadlin, Harvey Stewart, Jo Anne B. Strong, Harry H. Suber, Walter Taylor, Jr., Harry Ulmer, Catherine H. White, Cliff Wilson, D.M.D., and Judy Zane. Plus, the lawyers who are also members of the families of pioneer women lawyers: Minerva Wilson Andrews, Elizabeth C. Carpenter, Robert Galloway, III, Frampton W. Toole, Jr., William J. Rivers, III.

To a company of helpers: Carolyn Davis, Director, Bar Admissions Office, Dudly Autio, M.D., Fannie Autio, Dr. Mary Baskin-Waters, Jack Bass, James. E. Carson, M.D., Conchita Fielding, Ralph M. Ford, Dr. Belinda Gergel, Dr. Herbert Hartsook, Anne Marsha Knapper, Ed Knapper, Betty Lancer, R. Lavern Livingston, M.D., Dr. Amy Thompson McCandless, Layton McCurdy, M.D., Sandra K. McKinney, Dr. Nan Morrison, William L. Mulbry, M.D., Kenneth W. Shortridge, Jr., Josephine F. Shular, David M. Thiem, C.P.A., and to the South Carolina Bar Foundation, South Carolina Women Lawyers Association, the librarians and library resources of this state. I thank you all.

Introduction

Opportune circumstances occurred enabling this history to be researched, written and published in the early twenty-first century. Members of the South Carolina Women Lawyers Association first began the study, and I was fascinated by the subject. Facing my seventh decade, I wanted to lower my stress level in my law practice. When the South Carolina Bar Foundation offered a grant for research related to the legal profession, it was a propitious moment to combine my interest and my professional goals.

During the nineteenth century and into the twentieth, while women sought admission to the bar, the epithet "Portia" was universally applied. The dramatic appeal of the Shakespearean allusion has always intrigued me; thus, "Portia" became the prevailing metaphor of my book. The cast of characters was the women lawyers whose names were copied in chronological order from the records of the South Carolina Supreme Court. The two enrollment books used in this research were *Solicitor's Roll Commencing April 1809* and *Roll of Attorneys of South Carolina Beginning June 5, 1950.*

I have elected to divide the biographies of these 128 attorneys by the decade admitted to the bar. To examine our professional lives in terms of the decade in which we became lawyers is not to be taken lightly. Before embarking on this study, I assumed that our admission date was just a roll of the dice and out we came into a world we never made. Fitting into that world meant latching onto a chunk of the space-time-environmental gradient and treating it as our own. True, but to be successful, newly minted female attorneys had to accept the particular circumstances where we found ourselves and adapt our law practice accordingly. We had to accommodate our clients' perception of a good lawyer. The clients did not have to adapt to ours. We had to gain their confidence and establish trust before we could expect to be paid for services rendered. To do this required more than a law degree. It meant, among other things, to be comfortable in preserving private information, to understand financial matters, to endure conflicts, and to be on a par with the opposing attorney. The socioeconomics of each decade were significant to the way the new female barrister conducted herself vis-à-vis her colleagues and her clients. Thus, the decade in which a woman started her practice will symbolically be a home for her, a home she will carry with her always like the shell of a loggerhead turtle on a Carolina coastal island.

Although the history of women attorneys can be found in every century of American history, the legal profession in this state benefitted from steps taken in other states by pioneer Portias. The history of South Carolina women attorneys officially began February 14, 1918. The "sisters-in-law" of the teens and twenties rode in on the first wave of American feminism.

The third chapter shows how Portias of the 1930s struggled and sometimes succeeded under the weight of the Great Depression. World War II was a turn of events that opened almost all workplaces to women, as described in chapter four. This change stepped up the acceptance of professional women as equals. Chapter five explains the retrogressive 1950s, which shaped the disorderly 1960s of chapter six. The concluding chapter covers only the first four years of the seventies. It is an arbitrary cutoff based on the reality of the situation. By the mid-seventies, women were no longer an anomaly in the legal profession. They were numerous, they were competent, and above all they were taken for granted—a status they had been seeking for more than half a century.

*Artist unknown, Portia, Nineteenth century engraving,
3.75" x 5.25" (9.5 x 3 cm), private collection, Morris
Cohen, Yale Law Art Collection*

———

*The Quality of Mercy is not Strained
It Droppeth as the Gentle Rain from Heaven
Upon the Place beneath; it is twice Bless'd;
It Blesseth him that gives and him that takes.
~ William Shakespeare
"Merchant of Venice," Act IV, Scene I*

———

~ One ~

Before We Were Allowed

From 1903 to 1920, Frances (Fanny) Britton Wilson practiced law clandestinely in Rock Hill, South Carolina, with her father, William Blackburn Wilson, II, and her brother, W. Blackburn Wilson, III. Certainly she knew that the Supreme Court of South Carolina did not recognize her license from Pennsylvania, but she had the determination of Shakespeare's Portia, if not the dramatic flair.

The intrepid heroine of Shakespeare's "Merchant of Venice," disguising herself as a young male lawyer, defended her husband's benefactor against Shylock's demand for a pound of flesh. Failing to soften Shylock by appealing for mercy, she outwitted him. That stellar performance concluded Portia's career. Fanny Wilson, however, never practiced before the bar; instead, she devoted her adult life to essential, painstaking legal preparations. Patience and persistence were her forte. She lived a lifetime of "lawyering," following a small, but determined phalanx of her sex.

Reminiscing, Wilson remembered that in the early years of her practice, there was a constant pressure to meet deadlines. She recalled driving a horse-drawn buggy back from the railroad station at 1 A.M. after putting a brief on the day's final mail train, the last clear chance to get it to the printer in Columbia in time for a big case.

Frances Wilson was born in York County on November 25, 1880, the daughter of William Blackburn Wilson, II, and Mary Frances Britton. When Fanny, as she was called, was about eleven years old, her father had a law office in the county seat of York. He would bring home his notes for drafting of pleadings. According to the *Rock Hill Evening Herald* on May 13, 1952:

> There were no typewriters in general use. There were no stenographers in law offices, there were no 'scriveners' or trainer draftsmen such as the lawyers of England were accustomed to call upon from the earliest times.
>
> Under a kerosene lamp, her father would write out the draft and pass it on to Mrs. Wilson. She would copy it and pass it on to one of the children to copy. The paper made its way around the large dining room table from parents to Arra Belle, to "Black," to William, to Oscar, to Fanny, to Louie, to Minnie, to Mary, to Margaret, and to Yorke, until enough copies had been made. Three of the children, Black, William, and Fanny, became lawyers. Letter presses were used in subsequent years, but not for legal papers, which had to be served on parties to action.

In 1895, when Wilson was fifteen, the first women enrolled in the undergraduate school at the South Carolina College in Columbia. One woman, Ella Rebecca Norris of Columbia, invaded the law school there in 1897, an event that was entirely too much for Professor Pope, who questioned her right to receive a degree. The faculty, after considerable discussion, ruled that the right to enter the department implied the right to receive a degree. Mrs. Norris, however, did not complete the law course, and there were no women graduates in law until 1918.

Fanny Wilson began her post high school education at Converse College and then graduated from Winthrop College in 1900 with a degree in literature. A family story preserved by her great-niece, Minerva Wilson Andrews, also an attorney, says that Wilson and her father discussed what she would do with her life. They agreed that because of her soft voice, she would probably not make a good teacher, and she was not at all domestic or good with her hands.

Finally, her father said, "Well, Fanny, I guess you will just have to be a lawyer and work with me." And so she did. With her father's encouragement, she attended the University of Pennsylvania Law School and graduated in the class of 1903, automatically becoming a member of the Pennsylvania Bar. She then joined the firm of Wilson and Wilson, her father and brother, located in Rock Hill. In 1907-1908, Wilson took a leave of absence from the firm and worked in the Supreme Court Library in Washington on *Scott & Beaman's Digest of Federal Statutes.* She took another leave in 1918-1919 to work under Horace L. Tighman, state director of United States Employment Service, in Columbia.

Wilson continued in her father's firm until he died in 1920. She then became a law clerk and secretary to Judge Charles A. Woods of the United States Circuit Court of Appeals, Fourth Circuit. She served in this position for three years until shortly before Judge Woods's death in 1923.

There is no record of Wilson's professional occupation from the death of Judge Woods until 1934 when she accepted a position with the United States Justice Department, which recognized her Pennsylvania license. During the Roosevelt administration, the Department of Justice became a haven for women lawyers. Wilson practiced law in the Civil Division of the Justice Department until her retirement in 1952.

In 1918, South Carolina passed the landmark legislation admitting women to the bar. However, Wilson never applied for admission to the South Carolina Bar and, thus, never established formal legal credentials in her native state. For reasons unknown, she chose to remain a behind-the-scenes person. In all probability, she quietly rejoiced February 14, 1918, when Governor Richard I. Manning signed Act 441 that states, "Women shall be allowed to practice law within the State of South Carolina under the same rules, regulations, and conditions prescribed for the men of this state."

Fanny Wilson's career is characterized by professionalism without aggressiveness. There were, however, many women, both before her time and after, who would not settle for less than peer status with male colleagues. Some had to compromise their goals. Others, by dint of personality and fortuity of circumstances, forwarded the legal and social acceptance of the female attorney.

A more "in your face" type of woman made history almost a century and a half before the American Revolution. The first woman to act as an attorney in America was Margaret Brent from a wealthy, land-owning family in England, who immigrated to St. Mary's Parish, Maryland, in 1638. A cousin of Lord Baltimore, she managed to get herself appointed as counsel to the governor. She did not have a license to be an attorney from the Crown or from the Colony. Brent shattered all the restrictions facing seventeenth-century women and clearly had no equal in the province, male or female. Since the colonists did not quite know what to call such a unique woman, they frequently addressed her, in person and in court, as Gentleman Margaret Brent. Court records show that her name figured in 124 cases in eight years.

Currently, the Margaret Brent Women Lawyers of Achievement Award is the highest honor given by the American Bar Association to a woman in the profession. According to the ABA's publication of August 2, 1998, five of these awards are given annually. These awards recognize and celebrate the accomplishments of women lawyers who have achieved professional excellence in their field, influenced other women to pursue legal careers, opened doors for women lawyers in a variety of job settings that are historically closed to them, or advanced opportunities for women within a practice area of the profession.

In the nineteenth century, South Carolina had another would-be Portia, the daughter of a distinguished Charleston jurist, Judge J. G. Grimke. One of her biographies is *The Grimke Sisters from South Carolina: Rebels Against Slavery,* by Gerda Lerner (Lerner 1967). Sarah, the elder daughter, was born November 26, 1792. When her brother, Thomas, was apprenticed to the law office of Langdon Cheves, Sarah revealed her ambition to become an attorney. She was willing and ready to be a trailblazer, but her father and her brother dashed her hopes. Aspirations crushed, she and her sister became nationally known lecturers for the abolition of slavery and the right of women to take part in public affairs. Judge Grimke was said to have remarked, "If Sarah had been a boy, she would have made the greatest jurist in the country."

The New York Times magazine on November 5, 1997, reported:

> *[United States Supreme Court Justice Ruth Bader Ginsburg] likes to quote from a letter by Sarah Grimke, the feminist and anti-slavery lecturer from South Carolina, who visited the Supreme Court in 1853. In the letter, Grimke says she was invited to sit in the chief justice's chair. 'As I took the place,' she wrote, 'I involuntarily exclaimed, "Who knows, but this chair may one day be occupied by a woman." The brethren laughed heartily. Nevertheless, it may be true prophecy.' At this point, Ginsburg pauses and looks at the audience. 'Today,' she says with a smile, 'no one would laugh at that prophecy.'*

George C. Rogers, Jr., in his book, *Generations of Lawyers, A History of the South Carolina Bar* (South Carolina Bar Foundation, 1992), stated that until the American Revolution, probably one-third of the attorneys in South Carolina received their legal education at the Inns of Court in London. The rest had read law in the office of a senior member of the bar in the colony. After the Revolution, virtually all "young men read law in the offices of a leading member of the bar . . . (and) it was the legal mentor rather than the parent who had the most influence on the professional development of his charge." Not until January 23, 1867, was the first chair of law established at South Carolina College in Columbia. Of course, no women were admitted.

In the Midwest, women made somewhat earlier headway toward acceptance in the legal profession. The *Chicago Legal News* reported in February 1869 that a woman was practicing law in a small town in Iowa. Under the headline "Female Lawyer," the reporter noted that this lawyer's office was located "in North English, Iowa County, Iowa," and her office displayed a sign in gilt letters, "Mrs. Mary E. Magoon, Attorney at Law." The newspaper story added that Mrs. Magoon "is having a good practice and is very successful as a jury lawyer." There is no record that she had been admitted to the Iowa

State Bar, but in some states at that time, law practice on the county level did not require admission to a state or territorial bar. However, South Carolina was not among those states. The fact that the *Chicago Legal News* mentions this woman's legal practice invites the question as to how many other women were practicing law in small towns without having been admitted to their state's bar, such as South Carolina's Frances Britton Wilson. Very few of these aspiring Portias will be recognized in history.

In June 1869, twenty-three-year-old Mrs. Belle Babb Mansfield passed the Iowa State Bar and officially became recognized as the first licensed woman lawyer in the United States. She took advantage of the slump in college enrollment during the Civil War and registered for law classes at Iowa Wesleyan College. Mrs. Mansfield studied law with her brother, who was also her classmate. She never actually practiced law; she and her husband had careers in academia. Mansfield's license to practice began an era of gradual, although uneven, change in modernizing the bar by the admission of women.

Two months after Belle Mansfield was admitted to the Iowa State Bar, Myra Bradwell, editor of the *Chicago Legal News* and wife of a Cook County judge, passed the Illinois Bar examination. Since she had published the story of Mary Magoon's law practice, her interest in the issue was evident. The Supreme Court of Illinois denied Bradwell's admission to the bar on the grounds that she was a married woman and therefore not responsible for her actions. The Supreme Court of the United States took *certiorari* of the case. Despite the fact that Bradwell's attorney-adversary did not appear for the oral argument, the Supreme Court held this case in abeyance for two years. When it finally rendered a decision on *In Re. Bradwell,* 83 US 130 (1873), seven of the eight members ruled against Bradwell, deciding that each state could set its own requirements for admission to the bar. By that time, the question was moot for Bradwell because, in the interim, the state of Illinois began to admit married women to the practice of law.

Bella Lockwood became the first woman to present an oral argument before the Supreme Court of the United States. She was forty-one years old when she graduated from the National University Law School in Washington, D.C., in 1873. Lockwood built a general solo practice specializing in claims against the government, in particular, veterans' pension claims. The firm under her leadership survived forty years. In an 1888 interview, Lockwood said, "I never make less than three thousand dollars a year." It is noteworthy that a judge of the District of Columbia Supreme Court at the time was earning four thousand dollars.

Early in her legal career, Lockwood retained another Washington attorney to move her admission to the practice of law before the Supreme Court of the United States. In October 1876, Chief Justice Morrison R. Wait delivered the opinion of the Court on her motion as follows:

> By the uniform practice of the Court from its organization to the present time, and by the fair construction of the rules, none but men are permitted to practice before it as attorneys and counselors. This is in accordance with immemorial usage in England, and the law and practice in the highest courts of the United States. . . . As this Court knows no English precedent for the admission of women to the bar, it declines to admit, unless there shall be more extended public opinion or special legislation.

Lockwood lobbied her case before Congress for two years until the special legislation was enacted. Then she rode a tricycle from her office to the courthouse. "Her efforts to be admitted to the Supreme Court Bar were considered amusing by Washington society. The headline on a Washington newspaper story read, 'The Chief Justice Squelched the Fair Applicant.' " Malvina S. Harlan, wife of Justice John M. Harlan, recorded these frivolous comments in her book, *Some Memories of a Long Life 1854-1911*. The case that gave Lockwood the opportunity to be the first female attorney to make an oral argument before the Supreme Court of United States was *Kaiser v. Stickney,* 131 US clxxxvii (1880), arising just four years after her admission. The issue in the Kaiser case was the validity of a trust deed used as security for a bank note.

Two southern states admitted women to the practice of law in the nineteenth century—North Carolina in 1878 and Virginia in 1894. Between these dates, Massachusetts admitted women in 1882. Just eight years later, Karen Berger Morello in *The Woman Lawyer in America: 1638 to the Present* (Morello 1986) recorded one of these early women attorneys complaining about news coverage of women lawyers as being oddities: "Newspapers publish and republish little floating items about women lawyers along with those of the latest sea serpent, the popular idea seeming to be that one is about as real as the other."

At the turn of the twentieth century, women lawyers were universally called Portias. Morello also reported that the number of women in Massachusetts who aspired to be lawyers began to increase to such an extent that by 1908, there was a Portia Law School established in Boston. Portia Law School began as an evening bar review school for women preparing to take the bar examination. The school was so popular that by 1919, Governor Calvin Coolidge authorized it to begin awarding a bachelor of laws degree. Until 1938, it educated women exclusively. In 1969, its name was changed to the New England School of Law.

By 1910, women could practice law in forty states, but Alabama was the only state in the Deep South to have the enabling legislation. In the early 1900s, a progressive movement developed, which was to improve the South, as well as the nation, in business, cultural affairs, and female accessibility to professions. This movement emerged in South Carolina in 1903 with legislation forbidding the employment of children under the age of ten years in factories, mines, or mills. The bill passed the General Assembly, largely due to the efforts of a group of Columbia women. The bill also passed despite intense lobbying against it by the textile industry. During this progressive period, the other southern states began to admit women to the bar.

Appendix E of the *Twenty-Ninth Annual Report* (1912) of the Georgia Bar Association contains a verbatim record of a symposium titled "The Admission of Women to the Bar." The first speaker,

Henry C. Hammond, paid for the legal education of his niece, Katharine F. Hammond, who was admitted to the South Carolina Bar on December 14, 1932. He was also related to a South Carolina woman attorney who was admitted in 1974, Adele Jeffords Pope. Selected quotes convey the disparity of opinions.

Judge Henry C. Hammond (Augusta)

Women at the bar . . . of course, we want women at the bar. We not only want them at the bar, but they ought to stand preeminently as members of the bar. Now, gentlemen, I want to ask you in all seriousness—you know this subject is one of profound concern to me— how can you logically and fairly draw the distinction between the things, which by your solemn mandate, you prohibit them from doing? Now, what is the dignity or mentality necessary to practice law and that required to hoe cotton, or to take it from the field to the factory and weave it into cloth? What is the difference in the amount of skill required in this present day to practice law and the amount required to raise a baby? That hasn't a thing in the world to do with it. It is not the doubt of their skill, but the truth of the business is—I am going to voice it—these men simply dread the competition. That is the truth about it. It is well enough to talk about keeping the ladies away from the turmoil and the strife and the battle of the forum, but it is all rot. They dread the competition, I tell you. Hamilton Douglas was sitting there a minute ago, talking about a woman in Atlanta who has a splendid collection agency. She can go down to the justice court and present her case and file her papers and do as well as anybody. Then why should women be denied the right to make an honest living? What is it about man, anyhow, that makes him, working side by side with a woman and doing exactly the same work, worth fifty percent more than a woman?

Another thing about it—I want to get responsibility off my shoulders. I think it is a mighty bad thing to have money passing between man and his wife anyhow. I think the woman ought to be able to earn just as much money as the man, so that she will not have to be petting him and honeying him up for the price of a silk dress. Let her have a chance to earn her own money and manage her own affairs. Then the whole thing will be based on the highest kind of sentiment.

Women would make the best lawyers in the world. They are far and above the highest mental ability at the bar . . . they would put you in bankruptcy. Your practice would not be worth a dollar and a half a month to you. . . . [I]f one were to open an office in Georgia, it would only be a short time until Roland Ellis would be her chief clerk. Gene Black would be her typewriter, and Luther Rosser would be her office boy. *(Laughter and applause.)*

The President

The next gentleman on the program . . . takes the other side of this question.

Mr. Roland Ellis (Macon)

Mr. President and gentlemen of the bar association, I state to you that those irreverent words, uttered with this spirit of bravado, are the badge of courage—they could not flow from the mouth of man who had a mother-in-law. (Laughter.) I lay the proposition without fear of contradiction, that the bar associations might continue until the end of time, and you will never find a man lay down the radical doctrine that he laid down this morning, unless he finds himself involuntarily in the enforced solitary condition that traitor to his sex occupies. (Laughter.) Have we no rights left? Oh, I tell you, this is something that touches us closely. It means our rights, and our bread, and our business, and hear me, men of the Georgia Bar, I do not propose to be dictated to by such a man as Henry Hammond. (Laughter and applause.)

This is an important matter and I have a made a few notes in order that I may be correctly quoted by the press, and I want every word to burn into the heart of hearts of the Georgia Bar. This is a crisis in Georgia's history . . . of a race whose one-time sport was to pat red brawn or bet sesterces upon its members' blood, we have nigh come to pass, where we are but the proud caretakers of poodles and the submissive bearers of suffragette banners. My one conclusive reason against the admission of women to the bar with man's consent, is that this means to surrender of the last palladium of the liberties of men. The history of our male ancestors tells us of the times when we were vested with the right to imprison or decapitate unruly or recalcitrant spouses. We all know our rights were gradually yielded by enervated forbears, until it was permitted to chastise them only with a stick, and how finally it came to pass that even the insufficient weapon should not exceed the thickness of a thumb. Women have invaded every field of men's activity, and have made him their constant and unreasoning prey. Begging to be permitted to extend upon our personal needs, only five percent of our own incomes, we are being slowly pressed to the wall. They have invaded the profession of medicine, and monopolize the science of manicuring, and the day is not distant when the starving masseur will see his last patron enter the prosperous parlor of the relentless masseuse. They are taking away our ancient and immemorial right to manipulate the ballot box and control conventions. . . . Alimony is about to beggar the ancient sex of Caesar and Ulysses . . . and so it goes on, ever diminishing rights for us; ever increasing usurpation for them. . . . [B]oth Jeanne D'Arc and Carrie Nation were militant enemies of our sex. . . . They smile at us, and send their husbands to whip us if we wink back. . . .

We must rally men—men of the Bar of Georgia. In this state, at least we have kept our profession as a refuge. It is an old and honored profession, and we constitute an ancient and respectable, though weakened sex. In it, we daily strive in forensic combat to settle causes by reason and precedent. Shall it come to pass that they shall be won by curves and complexions, and lost by our lack of pulchritude? Jury trials now have their grave defects, even the danger of a Darrow, if guilty, cannot approach the fundamental catastrophe, the grievous hour when languorous eye and scarlet lip shall deprive of liberty and property, or open-work stockings interpret the Constitution. . . . Trysts with judges and dates with jurors—yea even the danger of a timely caress to opposing male counsel—may undermine the bulwarks of a constitutional government. What court, what jury, what counsel would impale the precedents of jurisprudence, reverse the adjudications of ages, discard mere vain facts, and sit spineless on the critical hour of duty, either when hair shimmered and sun gold, and cheeks burgeoned with rose, or when, eyes shining with star-light lips, fall with the crimson of challenge, plead with the voice of a lute?

That the effect of such innovation upon our social structure would prove generally revolutionary and subversive of some of our most cherished traditions cannot be doubted. A condition that would permit the wail of a babe . . . to be answered with the news that court is yet in session and mother, counsel of the defendant, cannot come, would presage the proximity of race suicide.

Equally alarming will be the situation . . . where one in the thrilling touch and caressing voice, how destructive of all enthusiasm, will it be to discover that her bosom conceals a demurrer, that in her silken hose is a subpoena. . . . We must rally, brothers of the bar, for our own and country's sake . . . and defend the Ark of the Covenant. We must keep charge of the last masculine profession remaining in Georgia.

Mr. E. R. Black (Atlanta)

Now, some of you men who may have foolishly thought in your own minds that women be admitted to the bar have evidently not given it a serious thought. . . . There is not a man who would give the stroke of his wife's hand on his hair for the printed brief ever originated in a lawyer's brain. There is not a man who would swap the welcoming smile of his little daughter when he gets home for the best legal document ever framed. . . . Keep them where they are now . . .

Judge John L. Hopkins (Paper read by the secretary of the bar.)

. . . There are multitudes of women who have no home except that which they themselves made and maintain; and there are many who perforce grow unlovely in the bitterness of an unequal struggle for subsistence. These would be willing to get along with less compliment, I fancy, if they were provided with a fairer opportunity to earn their daily bread. If a woman can gain an honorable independence by practicing law, I say it is a shame to shut her out. . . . In relative importance, as vitally essential to society, the two grand professions of law

and medicine stand by side. Women have been admitted to the medical profession, and their work has vindicated the wisdom of the step. Why should they not be admitted to the other?

The President

Well, then, having been accused of suggesting the subject, I take the authority of withdrawing from your consideration any action whatever on the subject.

In spite of this symposium, four years later in 1916, the State of Georgia admitted women to the practice of law. When in 1918, South Carolina and Arkansas began to accept women at the bar, the American Bar Association began to admit women attorneys as members.

When *In Re: Bradwell* was decided in 1873, Arkansas passed Act No. 88, Section 760, specifically restricting admission to its bar as follows: ". . . every male citizen . . . shall be entitled to practice in the courts of this state . . ." This act was amended to omit the word "male" in 1917. From the date of the passage of the act, it was almost a year, January 1918, before the first women was qualified and sworn in by the Supreme Court of Arkansas.

During the late nineteenth and early twentieth centuries, Canadian and British women also sought the right to practice law. "If it were not that I set out to open the way to the bar for others of my sex, I would have given up the effort long ago," said the first Canadian woman barrister who was "called to the bar" in 1897. At the time this comment was made, she was at the ripe old age of twenty-three.

In December 1919, the English Parliament passed its Sex Disqualification Removal Act, but the first woman in the United Kingdom to qualify as a barrister did so in Dublin in 1921. The first one in England was not until 1922. For research material on the history of European women attorneys, see "Portia Ante Portias: Women of the Legal Profession in Europe, ca. 1870–1925" (*Journal of Social History*, Summer, 2000).

Meanwhile, Claudia James Sullivan of Chesterfield County was beginning her last semester at the South Carolina Law School in 1918. She was one of three women enrolled. A bright young man in Sullivan's class raised the legal issue that women were not entitled by birth to be citizens because they had no right to suffrage, ergo, they could not be licensed attorneys. Sullivan was not intimidated. With her friends on "our side," she went directly to her local senator, George Kershaw Laney of Chesterfield County, with the request for legislation establishing women's right to practice law. Laney introduced the legislation on January 22, and was the floor leader in getting it passed. This legislation—Act No. 441—read: "Women shall be allowed to practice law within the State of South Carolina under the same rules, regulations, and conditions prescribed for men of this state." Later, Sullivan remarked, "So we got our little bill passed . . . that was a lot of fun."

Under the headline "What Butterfly Legislators Did," *The News and Courier* reported on February 13, 1918, "There are three young women now taking law at the University of South Carolina under the same rules and regulations and by the same examination as applies to men."

A young woman attorney then working in the Haynsworth law firm in Greenville had a vested interest in this legislative action. She had already been admitted to the practice of law in California and was prepared to take the South Carolina Bar examination.

This twenty-three-year-old woman, James Margrave Perry, stood before the Supreme Court of South Carolina on May 3, 1918, to become the first licensed female attorney in this state. (Perry's father had named her for himself.) Sullivan was sworn in the following month on June 12.

At this time, no women were allowed to vote in federal elections, but a proposed amendment to the United States Constitution granting suffrage was then before Congress. The dramatic mode of agitation for its passage was by picketing the White House. In certain circles, demonstrations aroused public sympathy, especially when the picketers were arrested. Finally, in September 1918, President Woodrow Wilson withdrew his opposition and announced his support for the amendment. Two months later, with congressional approval, the issue of suffrage for women was sent to the state legislatures for ratification or rejection. A vast army of women in the United States was unified under the umbrella of working for suffrage, a movement that has become known as the first wave of feminism.

Many of the early proponents for the suffrage movement were women lawyers who were also seeking admission to their state bars.

The first women seeking admission to the bar of South Carolina supported women's suffrage by marching in parades down Columbia's Main Street and joining organizations that actively supported the cause. Their struggle to become licensed attorneys was concomitant with the first wave of feminism.

I believe the most compelling reason some members of the legal profession objected to the admission of women to the bar was because their whole sphere of thinking was attuned to revere and rely on precedents. No other profession is as bound to the status quo as are lawyers.

In the following biographies, the number to the left of the name of the attorney is the order that each was admitted to the bar. The name is printed exactly as that individual signed the Supreme Court book of enrollment.

(1) James M. Perry
admitted May 3, 1918
1895–1964

"Miss Jim" Perry was the first woman to be admitted to the practice of law by the Supreme Court of South Carolina. She was associated with the Haynsworth Law Firm of Greenville from 1918 until her death in 1964. Perry was elevated in 1937 to partnership in the firm, then named Haynsworth, Perry, Bryant, Marion, and Johnstone. Additionally, there were seven male associates.

Before her admission to the bar of this state, Perry had been admitted to practice law in California. According to the *Spartanburg Herald* on January 18, 1957, "My father was an advanced thinker, and he cultivated the idea of my going into the legal profession from my teens. I had always liked music and gardening, but when you hear anything often enough, it makes an impression on you. I suppose if I had been left alone, I would have pursued one of my hobbies." Her father, James Margrave Perry, was an attorney, but had never practiced. He owned a business college and was on the faculty of Greenville Woman's College, now Furman University. Her mother, Jeanne LeGal Perry, home-schooled Perry all except three years of her elementary and high school education. Perry graduated from Greenville Woman's College in 1913 at the age of eighteen, followed by her legal education at the University of California.

When Perry was asked by the *Greenville News* on April 20, 1956, to comment on being the first woman admitted to the bar of this state, she said ". . . (on) being the first woman to take the bar examination in this state, the examiners were fair, but the Supreme Court had 'no comment' to make on my being admitted and ignored mentioning the fact that I was a woman." Graduates of out-of-state law schools were required to take the examination.

The South Carolina Bar Association, meeting at the Cleveland Hotel in Spartanburg in August 1919, accepted twenty-one new members, including Miss Jim Perry, an event reported in the book *Generations of Lawyers: A History of the South Carolina Bar* by George C. Rogers, Jr. Upon Perry's admission, every member welcomed her by rising and applauding. Among those giving her a standing ovation was Ralph Kennedy Carson, a prominent Spartanburg attorney and former president of the State Bar Association. Two months earlier, his daughter, Alice, had graduated from law school at New York University and intended to join her father's firm.

Articles in the *Greenville News* have described Perry's practice as "corporation lawyer and does only civil practice, deals principally with the organization and financing of corporations, taxes, wills probate matter, wage stabilization, the wages and hours law, and other government regulations."

"Miss Jim did all our trusts," brags Betty E. Dendy, who has been on the Haynsworth staff since 1956. Dendy also says that Miss Jim wore neutral colors, mostly gray, navy, and black. Her clothes were plain and she often wore tailored suits and a hat. Frances Smith, who was clerk of the Supreme Court of South Carolina (1959–1983), says Perry was the only attorney during her term that wore a hat while in oral argument before the court. In the course of Perry's career, she served as president of the local bar association, vice president of the National Association of Women Lawyers, and was a member of Kappa Beta Pi honorary legal society and many civic organizations.

(2) Claudia James Sullivan
admitted June 12, 1918
1895–1990

Claudia James Sullivan is undoubtedly the person to whom all South Carolina women lawyers are most indebted, including Miss Jim Perry. She initiated the change in policy, which previously had denied women's admission to the law school at the University of South Carolina. Not only was she the first woman to graduate from the law school, but she also triggered the legislation that allowed women to practice law in this state, as related earlier in this chapter.

In a letter written to her niece in 1969, Sullivan responded to the inquiry about her gaining entrance to law school as follows:

> There were several women who entered the law school after I did, but I had all the fun. You see, when I decided to enter law school, I just went out to the dean's office with my usual assurance that it would be easy. Well, the dear Dean Baker was very nice about it, but firm—no women were allowed to register for the school of law. So, I was firmly, but gently, disposed of. Walking back through the state house grounds, I decided to drop in on some of my new friends. When discussing my turn down, this man (I'd rather not name him even yet) said, 'Why you really mean this, don't you?' I said, 'Sure.' So he got a gleam in his eye and said, 'You wait here a minute. I think I can help you and at the same time jolt some folks into the twentieth century.' Pretty soon, he was back and handed me a sheet of paper. He said, 'When you go back to register, just hand the dean this paper and when time comes to get yourself sworn in, I'll be there to cheer you on.' A few days later, I went back to call on the dean. When he patiently explained to me that women were not allowed to enter the

school of law, I handed him the neatly folded paper. He opened it, glanced at it, and said with a kind-of half grin, 'Please wait here,' and disappeared. Soon, he was back. He gave me back my paper and asked me to come with him so we could settle this matter. At a faculty meeting, the dean presented my application and one rather grim looking professor asked me (and not too kindly) what gave me the idea that I had the right to make such a request. My answer, 'I am white, of good character, and have the proper credits.' That dear dean said, 'Read them your paper now.' Everybody stopped talking and I read it. (It was fun to read it—I made history for at least thirty seconds.) 'Article So and So, Section So and So: Women are hereby permitted to enter ALL Schools of the university.' After a short silence (you could hear the traditions of the elders splintering) it was decided that there was nothing else to do except let me register.

Since 1867, when the law school was established, all graduates were exempt from taking the bar examination and were admitted to the practice on what was known as the "diploma privilege." As noted in the case of Perry, this is not the case with out-of-state graduates.

Sullivan's great-nephew, Florence attorney William J. Rivers, III, has her historical artifacts, her 1918 law school diploma, the original of her 1969 letter, and her original Supreme Court license to practice law.

Not a rabble-rouser, the description of Sullivan in the 1919 college yearbook, *Garnet and Black,* says, "Miss Sullivan is just one of the fellows—witness the nickname Jim. Flits about the campus chattering like a jaybird, saucy as a wren, and self-assertive as an eagle. Chafes under conventions and chimes in over every conversation. . . . [T]he only branch of law that will be of service to her is that of domestic relations."

Sullivan was the daughter of James and Melinda Horn Sullivan of Ruby, Chesterfield County. Her father was a boilermaker for cotton gins and her mother was a schoolteacher. "She was an adventuresome person," says her niece, Thelma Venters. The year after Sullivan's graduation, she married Charles Meredith Boyd, and they lived their entire married life in Florida, primarily in Miami, where she practiced real estate law. At some time during her adult life, she legally changed her middle name to "Jimmy." The couple retired to Apopka, Florida, where she died on September 26, 1990.

(3) Minnie Layton Holman
admitted August 8, 1918
1881–1952

Minnie Holman, whose first name appears as Minna in certain records, was the first married woman attorney in South Carolina. Upon her admission to the bar, she became a partner with her husband, Alfred W. Holman, in the firm of Holman and Holman, with offices at 1223 Washington Street, Columbia. Holman entered law school the semester following Sullivan.

The 1919 college yearbook remarks that, "Mrs. Holman aspires to become a junior partner in the firm of Holman and Holman. When that happens, the senior member will become known as 'Mrs. Holman's husband.' So long as we continue to have men juries, Mrs. Holman will win ninety-nine percent of her cases. She will undoubtedly be the best married woman lawyer in South Carolina." Their firm was listed in the city directories from 1919 until 1935 when Alfred W. Holman became a Richland County judge. After 1935, she is no longer listed in the city directories as an attorney. Julia Kleckly knew Minnie Holman for many years, as both families were members of the Lutheran Church of the Incarnation in Columbia. Kleckly, however, did not know that Holman was, like herself, an attorney. Kleckly Tison was admitted to the practice of law in 1947.

(4) Julia David Charles
admitted December 6, 1918
1879–1940

Julia Charles, the fourth woman admitted to the bar of South Carolina, was the first to do so after preparing for the bar examination by reading law under the supervision of a member of the bar for a period of at least two years. To qualify to take the bar examination by reading law, students were also required to study an itemized list of textbooks as prescribed by Supreme Court rules. Beginning in 1912 and for six years thereafter, Julia Charles is identified in the *Greenville City Directory* as a stenographer and book-keeper for attorney William G. Sirrine. Presumably, she studied law in his office.

Charles opened her solo office at Room 301 Masonic Temple on South Main Street in Greenville. Her secretary, Anna McCants Beaty, began reading law in Charles's office just as Charles had done with Sirrine. After Beaty became an attorney in 1923, the two formed a partnership and became the first female law firm in the state, which lasted until Charles retired in 1940. In 1928, they took in a male associate, James H. Woodside, but within a few years, he left to accept a position as an administrator of the Home Building and Loan Association of Greenville.

Charles was a longtime member and secretary of the Board of Trustees of the Greenville City schools.

(5) Mary G. Sledge
admitted June 12, 1919
1880–1970

Mary Sledge practiced law for most of her professional life in a second floor office in the Agurs Building in her hometown of Chester. She was that county's first woman attorney and, at the time of her death, was the senior member of the Chester County Bar Association.

"She had a busy practice in real estate, wills, and probate work," recalls local historian, Ann Marion of Chester. "Miss Mary's office was in the center of town, across the street from the Confederate Monument, and just a few doors from the courthouse. Everybody knew her as a direct descendent of a Chester heroine, a pregnant Mrs. McKinney, who, in the 1700s, was scalped by the Indians and lived to tell it."

Sledge took her undergraduate education at Winthrop College and was thirty-nine years old when she enrolled in the law school at the university. After her admission to the bar, she worked for a short time with the Spartanburg firm of Nichols and Wyche and then with the Chester law firm of Glenn and McFadden before opening her solo practice.

Chief Justice (ret.) George T. Gregory, Jr., of Chester reports, "My aunts always used Mary Sledge for their attorney; she represented most all the school teachers in the county. When I was a neophyte lawyer, we called her Miss Mary, and she was a great lady."

(6) Alice Screven Carson
admitted November 21, 1919
1891–1981

In June 1919, Alice Carson graduated from the law school of New York University, one of six females in a class of twenty-six. One of her professors was a young, New York attorney, John McKim Minton, Jr., to whom she was married in March 1920.

Alice was the daughter of a prominent Spartanburg attorney, Ralph Kennedy Carson, and his wife, Catherine Bonneau Johnson. Alice graduated from Converse College with Julia Charles in 1910. Before she attended New York University Law School, she had earned a master's degree in history from Columbia University in New York. Between her admission to this state's bar and her marriage, Alice was associated with her father's law firm in Spartanburg.

Alice and John Minton made their home in New York, where he maintained a private practice. John also served as assistant district attorney and as a special state prosecutor. "She (Alice Carson Minton) did not practice law during her marriage, but I do vividly remember that Jack related every case to her on a daily basis and she certainly lived through a life of law in this way," says her goddaughter and cousin, Walton Carlisle Beeson.

Six women were admitted to the South Carolina Bar between 1918 and 1920. These women were the pioneers, but more were to follow. At least two others had begun preparing for the bar examination by reading law under the tutelage of a member of the bar, and several were preparing to register for law school. Although no paper trail has been found, in all likelihood, there were other women, in addition to Fanny Wilson, who were associated with a law practice, having received their legal education out of state, but who did not seek admission to the South Carolina Bar. In conclusion, it should be noted that to most aspiring Portias, this decade was labeled "Before we were allowed."

USC School of Law, 1918.
Claudia J. Sullivan on front row.
Minnie L. Holman on second row.

James M. Perry, 1918.

Claudia James Sullivan, 1918.

Minnie Layton Holman, 1918.

Mary G. Sledge, 1919.

Alice Screven Carson, 1919.

~ *Two* ~
Feme Covert and/or Feme Sole

Progressivism, as described in the previous chapter, some histo-
rians assert, enjoyed an Indian summer in the early 1920s. The most
notable example, of course, was the passage of the Nineteenth
Amendment, granting women suffrage. Not to be overlooked, however, was South Carolina's modification of the common law concept
of coverture for married women.

In the early twentieth century, a woman did not need to be
admitted to the bar to know that under the common law, a husband
and wife were one person and that one person was the husband. The
married status of a woman was known as feme covert. Under the
laws of coverture, she was unable to act as a legal person (i.e., her
contracts were void, not merely voidable). Her husband was liable for
her torts, and she was bound to obey him at peril of corporal pun-
ishment. Common law viewed this incapacitating status as a protection for women. An unmarried woman was a feme sole, including
one whose marriage had been dissolved by death. Feme soles were
under no such disqualifications as their married sisters.

On August 26, 1920, feme covert and suffragette Eulalie Salley
set off the Aiken fire alarm before the chief knew what was hap-
pening. This was a pre-arranged celebration of women's right to
vote. The suffragettes were in high spirits because the solons of

Tennessee had just voted to ratify the Nineteenth Amendment to the United States Constitution, bringing in the requisite number of states to give women the right to vote in federal elections. Salley, though not a lawyer, was married to one. In January of that year, the South Carolina Legislature had rejected this amendment. Enfranchising women was not popular in the Palmetto State.

At the 1920 annual meeting of the state bar, President P. A. Wilcox spoke against reform, particularly against the passage of the Eighteenth and Nineteenth Amendments to the United States Constitution: "There are two instances—prohibition and women suffrage—which can be peculiarly referred to as samples of assault. . . . [T]hey would not be successful but for the wave of hysteria, as the result of emotional excitement, consequent upon reaction from the world of conflict."

Less than eight months after the national suffrage amendment had been ratified, the legislature of this state passed an act conferring on women the right to vote in state elections. Actually, this "right to vote," for all practical purposes, applied only to Caucasians. South Carolina was then, and remained for another score or more years, virtually a one-party state—the Democratic Party. That party operated somewhat like a private club, excluding blacks from membership. Not until the 1940s did the federal courts require the Democrats to register black voters. Suffrage, however, gave the female attorneys (all white) a useful tool. They now were able to be notary publics, a privilege reserved only for those registered to vote. Almost every legal document, pleading, affidavit, and paper that crosses a lawyer's desk must be notarized.

The act granting women the right to vote in state elections, however, was followed shortly by another act that specifically excluded women from jury service. At the time, juries were drawn from registered voters. In his 1998 book, *South Carolina: A History,* published by the University of South Carolina Press, Walter Edgar noted, "The supporters of this latter legislation believed 'respectable women had no real desire to be jurors,' and it was the duty of the elected officials to 'protect the weaker sex from the unpleasantness of jury duty' " (Edgar 1998).

During the progressive period of the first decades of the twentieth century, the South Carolina Supreme Court and Legislature took tentative steps toward the emancipation of married women. The case of *Edwards v. Wessinger*, 65 SC 161, 43 S.E. 518 (1903), laid down some rules with reference to the liability of the husband for the torts of his wife. The case of *Prosser v. Prosser*, 114 SC 45, 102 S.E. 787 (1919), held that a wife could bring an action in tort against her husband for an assault and battery. The first radical departure from the common law, however, came in some 1922 legislation that read: "When a married woman is a party, her husband must be joined with her, except that: 1. When the action concerns her separate property, she may sue or be sued alone."

This act was repealed and re-enacted in 1925, giving the married woman larger liberties and corresponding responsibilities. It provided:

A married woman may sue and be sued as if she were unmarried: Provided that neither her husband nor his property shall be liable for any recovery against her in any such suit; but judgment may be enforced by execution against her sole and separate estate in the same manner as if she were sole. When the action is between herself and her husband, she may likewise sue and be sued alone.

It would be another thirteen years before the Supreme Court of this state actually recognized the full emancipation of married women.

In this decade of the 1920s, legal education was also a beneficiary of late-blooming reform. The University of South Carolina Law School's three-year, six-semester program was enacted, and its admission policy was changed to require two years of undergraduate study. Actually, these changes were made to enable the school to meet accreditation standards of the American Association of Law Schools. Until the fall of 1922, the law school curriculum was two years (four semesters), and admission could be made directly after high school graduation. Daniel Walker Hollis commented on the bar association's reaction to these changes in Volume II of his 1956 book, *University of South Carolina,* published by the University of South Carolina Press:

> In its efforts to raise standards, the law faculty also ran into oppo-
> sition from some members of the bar. Scores of successful attorneys who
> practiced law on the basis of a high school diploma and a two-year
> LL.B. stubbornly opposed initiation of a program that would require
> at least five years of training at the college level.
>
> They argued that two years of academic work plus a three-year
> course were obviously unnecessary, when South Carolina lawyers by
> the score had succeeded without such training. The rules for admission
> to the bar were another source of disagreement. Although graduates of
> the law school since its establishment in 1867 had been admitted
> without examination, some attorneys objected to the 'diploma privi-
> lege' (Hollis 1956).

Furman University had already opened a law school in 1921, which met national accreditation standards. Students could earn a bachelor of arts degree after completing three years of the academic program and three years of law study. This law school fell on hard times during the Great Depression and closed, transferring its students to Duke University.

In spite of the advances in women's rights and progress in raising educational requirements for lawyers, popular images bring up a glamorized vision of the "Roaring Twenties"—bath tub gin, flappers, the Charleston, *The Great Gatsby.* The accessibility of the automobile was economic progress that eventually stimulated a whole new area of legal services; however, stark reality in South Carolina during this decade was economic distress. During the first six months of 1921, cotton prices were around forty cents a pound; prices began to drop and by December, cotton was thirteen and one-half cents a pound. Hard times combined with strict adherence to biblical precepts, as interpreted by most South Carolina churches, did not translate into the glitter so frequently associated with this decade. The eleven would-be Portias, whose biographies follow, were breaking traditions, as did their predecessors described in the previous chapter; however, they were certainly not "flappers."

(7) Evelyn C. Marcus
admitted May 22, 1920
1887–1963

Evelyn Marcus was the first disabled woman attorney in this state and the first woman attorney in Orangeburg County. Due to a genetic disorder, she was profoundly hearing impaired; however, she read lips competently. The *Orangeburg Times and Democrat* reported on May 25, 1920:

> *Miss Evelyn Marcus, of this city, was admitted to the practice of law on Saturday by the South Carolina Supreme Court following an examination in Columbia.*
>
> *Miss Marcus is the first woman of this county to be admitted to the bar and is among the very few women of this state who have had the same distinction.*
>
> *She was born in this city and is the daughter of the late Mr. and Mrs. M. Marcus and has a brother, Joe Marcus, in this city. It is her intention to practice her profession in this city of her birth.*

Her clients were other lawyers, remembers her nephew, Milton Marcus. "She maintained an office and did work for other lawyers." There were no other attorneys in the Marcus family, and she did not attend law school. It is not known in whose office she learned to read law or if she had an undergraduate education. Attorney C. Walker Limehouse, who began the practice of law in Orangeburg in the 1930s, has no recollection that she had a law office since his time as an attorney.

(8) Tressie Jean Pierce
admitted June 8, 1921

In the 1920s, almost all secretaries, called typewriters, were male; however, Tressie Jean Pierce was one of the first female secretaries in this state's legal profession. Pierce was also in the last class to graduate from law school with four semesters in two years. While in law school, she was a stenographer in the Columbia law office of Barrett and McDonald.

Pierce's first position as an attorney was in the Federal Land Bank of Columbia. Following that, she became a law associate at the law firm of Lyles and Lyles at 1011 National L. & E. Building, also in Columbia. At the time, William H. Lyles was president of the State Bar Association.

In 1922, Pierce formed a partnership with newly sworn attorney Sue Evelyn Lester that lasted two years. Their office was located at 7 Clark Law Building in Columbia. After the dissolution of the partnership, Pierce continued in solo practice at 1233 Washington Street, Columbia, near the office of Minnie Layton Holman, Esquire, whose office was at 1223 Washington Street. After 1934, Pierce is no longer listed in the *Columbia City Directory*.

(9) Sue Evelyn Lester
admitted June 14, 1922
1892–1962

Sue Evelyn Lester became the first woman attorney in this state to defend an accused in a jury trial for murder. She won an acquittal in that case. Another first to her credit—she became the first woman attorney to appear in the United States federal courts of this state.

Lester was the former Sue Evelyn Barnes of Spartanburg, who attended the Columbia College for Women, Converse College, and by age sixteen, had graduated from Lynwood College in North Carolina. She was married and had two daughters before she entered law school at the university in Columbia. This background information was reported in *The State* on June 12, 1923, which noted additionally that her husband was a well-known theater owner in Columbia. The article read, "While a student at the university, she was one of only five members of the McIver Legal Honor Club, the highest academic society in the law school." The 1922 issue of the *Garnet and Black* yearbook said of her ". . . [T]hough her time is occupied with her home, children, husband, and large business interests, she has distinction in her class."

Upon her admission to the bar, Lester formed a law partnership with Tressie Jean Pierce, which lasted two years. Then she ran unsuccessfully for a seat in the state House of Representatives. In the same year, Lester opened her own office at 1438 Main Street, Columbia, over the Rialto Theater, where she continued a solo practice until 1961.

The *Newsview,* a weekly South Carolina news magazine, in its issue of June 27, 1936, reported her other unsuccessful bid for public office:

> Last fortnight, heavyset Mrs. Lester announced again [that she will run] for the House of Representatives. Said bobbed-haired, widowed Mrs. Lester, 'There's very little money in law for women. There are too many illiterate and semi-illiterate persons in South Carolina who still think (a woman's) women's place is in the home.'

(10) Ila Salley Reamer
admitted June 14, 1922
1882–1958

Ila Salley Reamer had the distinction of being academically first in the law school class of 1922; she also was a member of Phi Beta Kappa and the McIver Legal Honor Club. Reamer used her legal education exclusively for public service as a charter member of the South Carolina League of Women Voters, as chairman of the University Board of Visitors, and as a member of the Board of the Department of Public Welfare. During World War II, she served on the county food rations board. The 1922 *Garnet and Black* yearbook described her as "mental brilliance not to be expected from one who has such varied interest as mother, housekeeper, and 'ward heeler'," (one who delivers the votes from her political ward).

Before entering law school, she married Cornelius Youmans Reamer, president of Reamer Ice and Fuel Company, and they had two children. A granddaughter, Nela Gibbons, says Reamer's husband "Didn't care what she did so long as she didn't work for a fee."

Reamer proudly marched down Main Street in Columbia supporting women's suffrage, but she would not march down Main Street in support of prohibition.

The State reported on June 13, 1922, "Mrs. Reamer lives so near the university, at 1507 Pendleton Street, that she can't keep away from the campus and collegiate halls and is constantly taking some course or the other. A couple years ago, she decided that, as a knowledge of the law is frequently useful and the process of attaining it is good mental training . . . she got more and more interested in the subject and with every examination, she pulled down the stars."

Reamer was a graduate of Winthrop College and by 1913, she had earned a master's degree in economics from the University of South Carolina. After she graduated from the law school, she earned a doctor of philosophy in economics from the university.

(11) Ann McCants Beaty
admitted May 26, 1923
1901–1966

Ann Beaty, who on some occasions spelled her name "Anna," and Julia David Charles, admitted in 1918, formed the first female law firm in this state. Beginning in 1923, they maintained a successful Greenville practice for at least two decades. After Charles withdrew from the firm in the 1940s, Beaty maintained the office until 1960.

Before Beaty became a law partner, she was a secretary for Charles while at the same time reading law to prepare for the bar examination. Both women's interest in becoming attorneys originated while they worked in the office of William G. Sirrine, Esquire.

It is noteworthy that, to prepare for the bar exam, Beaty had done more than read law in the office; she enrolled in the then-new law school at Furman University. She is pictured in their 1924 yearbook and was that school's only female student. Before completing all the courses for graduation, she took the bar examination, passed, and decided not to continue at the law school.

"Their practice was chiefly 'real estate' and they were successful," recalled J. D. Todd, Jr., of the Greenville Bar. By 1928, Beaty was president of Cherry Investment Company, secretary of Lincoln Cemetery Association, secretary and treasurer of Cherry Development Company, and secretary and treasurer of River Falls Realty Company.

In the June 26, 1931, *Yorkville Enquirer,* the editor wrote that Beaty said, " 'The other lawyers at home treat us well, and very courteously'. Their firm declines criminal practice and very seldom has jury cases in court, most of their practice being in the chancery side of the courts, cases tried by judges." Editor Alfred M. Grist continued, "But at a term of court at Spartanburg, she was treated very shabbily, disdainfully, and discourteously by both bench and bar, and she remarked that evidently the court found feminine attorneys a novelty to be frowned down upon, while at Greenville, everyone is accustomed to them. She explained that the path by women lawyers here has been made much harder to travel by some of the women admitted to the bar who aped men in clothes and voice and tried to act like tough hombres; this caused an almost insurmountable prejudice against the women lawyers who are cultured ladies as well."

Subsequently, the daughter of the *Yorkville Enquirer* editor was admitted to the bar of this state in 1945.

(12) Kate Montgomery Brodnax
admitted June 14, 1923

Kate Brodnax enjoyed the distinction of being the only law student in this study who ever successfully differed with the dean of the school. This tantalizing detail was reported in the university's *Garnet and Black* without any additional explanation. While a law student, she was always on the Honor Committee. Her class was the last one to graduate after four semesters (two years).

Kate Montgomery, originally from Marion, was in the class of 1904 at Winthrop College. After graduation from Winthrop, she married Frank Brodnax and was a professor at Shelton College before she entered law school. The university's yearbook for 1923 titillates by mentioning her successfully challenging the dean, and adds this salute, ". . . we envy her wonderful grades." After graduation, Brodnax did not remain in Columbia and how she used her legal education is not known.

(13) Maude Baker
admitted June 10, 1925
1892–1987

Maude Baker of Kingstree primarily focused her legal career around the seventy-eight acres in Williamsburg County that she purchased when she was only twenty-six years old. Not only did she have her own home built on the land, but she also built one for her family and one to sell, subdividing most of it into lots, and serving as the seller and as the seller's attorney. This property was located near the run of Broad Swamp and west of Main Road.

Four years later, around the time Baker entered law school, an interesting event occurred in Williamsburg County—three hundred women voted. Since no other county in South Carolina at that time matched the voter participation of the women in this rural county, the fact is reported in Walter Edgar's *South Carolina: A History*. Unfortunately, the author was unable to verify any role Maude Baker may have played in this enthusiasm for women's suffrage. However, her sister, Lil Baker Cash, believes Maude and their mother participated. "They believed that every woman should vote."

The daughter of William Pressley and Ida Johnson Baker, Maude was born in Clarendon County and was the first of eight children. She decided to go to law school while she was working in the Kingstree law office of Kelly and Hinds. At the time she was admitted to the bar, Florida was having booming land sales. She moved there and earned her living abstracting the titles to lots for sale, returning to South Carolina after the death of her father in 1929.

Her obituary in the March 11, 1987, issue of *The News*, the county newspaper, states:

> She was a graduate of Kingstree High School and Draughn's Business College. After working as a bookkeeper for several years, she

returned to pursue a law degree. She enrolled in the University of South Carolina Law School and graduated in 1925. . . . She practiced law first in Orangeburg and later in Kingstree. . . . Miss Baker also worked for the Exchange Bank of Kingstree and several other area businesses as a bookkeeper.

Baker's Kingstree office was on the second floor at the corner of Academy and Main Streets. Her real estate investment was first referred to as the "Maude Baker Tract," and she became known as "Miss Maude."

In the late 1990s, local lawyer William M. O'Bryan recalled that he knew her, but did not realize that she was also an attorney. O'Bryan believed, "Folks thought she was some kind of an eccentric because she hung out her wash clothes on Sunday and never owned an automobile. An eccentric introvert, but pleasant."

"After World War II, many people here were needing building lots and this is when she sold most of her property," O'Bryan said. "She put restrictions on the subdivision and named it Colonial Heights." The property is now within the city limits of Kingstree and includes seventeen blocks of homes. In November 2001, James M. Connor, a local attorney, said, "Some of that property is still in her estate. Once, she bought a pick-up truck and she would drive it as far as Highway 52, park it, and then get out and walk the rest of the way to her destination. She would not drive across that highway." Her sister, Lil, admits, "She never had a driver's license."

In Maude's later years, she would take the great nephews and nieces for Sunday walks and teach them to identify tree leaves and plants, just as her mother had done for Maude and her siblings.

(14) Mary S. Wilburn
admitted December 21, 1927
1901–1966

Upon Mary S. Wilburn's admission to the bar, she became an attorney in the state's first female firm, Charles and Beaty of Greenville, where she remained for seven years. Wilburn had previously been a secretary in this firm. While there, she had read law in preparation for taking the bar examination.

Wilburn left the firm to take a position as secretary to the treasurer of Furman University. From 1943 to 1958, she was secretary to attorney Dennis B. Leatherwood. Wilburn concluded her career as a United States probation officer, a post she held until she qualified for retirement.

(15) Martha Black Wallace
admitted February 17, 1928

Martha Wallace, also known as Mrs. E. Barton Wallace, may have been known as a sheriff. In her senior year, the *Garnet and Black* yearbook identified her as a sheriff as well as a law student. Prior to beginning her legal education, Wallace and her husband were residents of Columbia, but this writer does not believe that she was sheriff of Richland County. At that time, some cities in South Carolina had sheriffs who had limited responsibilities, such as collecting water bills. No record has been found to substantiate this, but Wallace may have been a city sheriff. Two years after Wallace was admitted to the bar, she was listed as E. Barton Wallace, attorney at law, with an office at 1207 Washington Street, Columbia. Four years later, she was no longer listed as an attorney in Richland County in the city directories.

(16) Alice Robinson
admitted June 11, 1929
1904–1989

Alice Robinson had a long and distinguished association with her Columbia family law firm. She was the daughter of David W. Robinson, a leader in the State Bar Association, who had founded a prominent trial law firm in the nineteenth century. Her father and two brothers were associated with the firm. A position was waiting there for Alice upon her admission to the bar. She and her two siblings had grown up with their father's law books and the *Southeastern Digest of Supreme Court* cases in their living room. Her undergraduate studies were at Randolph-Macon College in Virginia. She studied law at the University of South Carolina. As a member of the family firm, Alice primarily served real estate clients. In 1940, she married a professor of civil engineering, Reuben C. Johnson. She changed her last name for social purposes, but did not change her name professionally. "She was very popular with her lady clients; they just flooded to her," remembers her sister-in-law, Bessie Boykin. Julius W. McKay, Esquire, recalls that Alice always advised her women clients not to sign away their dower without some consideration, thereby clouding lots of titles to real estate and making a strike for women's rights.

Members of her firm give Alice full credit for successfully holding their law practice together during World War II while its male partners were serving in the military.

(17) Emmie Kirven
admitted June 11, 1929
1902–1997

Emmie Kirven did not go to law school to become an attorney, and she never practiced law. She claimed to have gone to law school "just to prove that I could do it."

Kirven was the daughter of John K. and Anna Blackwell Kirven, who owned about two thousand acres of land in Darlington County. Her undergraduate degree from the University of South Carolina was in civil engineering. Kirven's Darlington County death certificate notes that her occupation was "manager of real estate." "I don't think she ever worked a day in her life outside of her farming and real estate interest," says her nephew, Dr. Cliff Wilson.

Four months after Robinson and Kirven were admitted to the bar, it was Big Thursday, South Carolina's annual classic gridiron game between the South Carolina and Clemson football teams. This tradition originated at the 1896 State Fair and gained momentum each year. Going into the 1929 game, Clemson was undefeated and Carolina had only one loss. Each team was under consideration for the Southern Conference Championship. Fourteen thousand screaming spectators sandwiched into an old wooden stadium at the state fair grounds in Columbia. Tension was so high that no one was aware that the stock market was collapsing. The crowd watched as Clemson scored a touchdown to break a tie and take the game with a score of 21-14.

This particular Big Thursday turned out to be Black Thursday, setting off an economic crisis so serious that the state's financial structure collapsed. It would be four years before another woman graduated from the university's law school.

Sue Evelyn Lester, 1922.

Ila Salley Reamer, 1922.

Maude Baker, 1925.

Martha Black Wallace, 1928.

Alice Robinson, 1929.

~ Three ~

Portia's New Deal

The Great Depression of the 1930s was a bleak period, impoverishing professionals and wage earners alike. The average annual income, if a family had one, was between five hundred and one thousand dollars. In an effort to reduce government personnel, Congress passed an act stipulating that any married woman living with her spouse would be the first to be dismissed, and married women would get the lowest consideration for future employment in civil service. The number of marriages dropped forty percent from the previous decade.

Despite the less than glowing economy, a total of fourteen South Carolina women obtained admission to the state bar between 1930 and 1938. A significant factor in the advancement of women in the legal profession was the election of Franklin D. Roosevelt as president of the United States on November 8, 1932. Not only did he appoint the first woman to serve in a presidential cabinet, but he also implemented a program called the New Deal, creating the largest federal government in history. The Roosevelt administration was distinctive in its search for a more inclusive, plural definition of America. One result of the growing acceptance of women in government was a striking increase in employment of women lawyers by the Department of Justice. For the female barrister seeking success in any type of practice, this was an encouraging development. It was during the 1930s that South Carolina's Fanny Wilson became an attorney in the Department of Justice, as previously mentioned. She was, by that time, an experienced lawyer with prestigious references. Grace White, a neophyte straight out of law school, was turned down by the Justice Department, as will be described in her own words later in this chapter. There was opportunity for some women in this decade, but for many, it was a struggle for existence.

Anecdotes about the practice of law in Charleston during the Great Depression spotlight hard times. On Saturday, most lawyers kept their offices open all day and courthouses were open until one in the afternoon. No trial courts were in session from May until late September. B. A. M. Moore, a leading attorney, was heard to say that he feared his family would starve if he couldn't try a case during those summer months. As late as the 1950s, I heard stories about lawyers in the 1930s stationing someone at the office of the recorder of deeds during a real estate closing. This person was to check for last-minute judgments and to see if the seller or mortgagor was try-ing to sell or mortgage the property twice in one day.

About the only bright spot for attorneys during this time was in foreclosure and bankruptcy actions, and there were many of them. For these proceedings, the court costs and lawyer's fees were paid first if there was any money to be distributed. Most lawyers had a secretary to whom they could not pay a salary and who worked just to have something to do. To save money on utility bills, attorneys did not turn on office lights unless it was necessary. Augustine T. Smythe, Esquire, would tell his stenographer, "Daughter, don't turn on the office light unless you are typing."

During Roosevelt's first hundred days in office, the Federal Housing Act was enacted to make federally insured loans available to homeowners. These insured loans multiplied the number of home-owners in South Carolina, putting bread and meat on the tables of real estate lawyers like Greenville's firm of Charles and Beaty. The Farm Credit Act, also passed in the first hundred days, made loans available to farmers for seed money in exchange for giving a mortgage on a piece of personal property, such as a tractor.

Thirty years later, the Justice Department directed district attorneys to foreclose on unpaid notes that were given under the Farm Credit Act. Arthur G. Howe, assistant district attorney of the Carolina low country, began these actions by sending all the farmers a letter of intent. Several days after Howe's letters were mailed, I noticed a muddy-colored pickup truck parked in front of the federal courthouse. The driver, smelling of manure, was wearing his field clothes, overalls, and a baseball hat. In the bed of his truck was a mule, the same color as the truck. The farmer asked Broad Street lawyer Lloyd Wilcox the way to Howe's office and showed the lawyer Howe's demand to repossess the mule he had given as security for seed money. Wilcox delighted in telling Howe to look out of the window and see what was waiting for him to feed.

By 1935, the New Deal included the Work Progress Administration Act and the Social Security Act. WPA employees built and renovated public buildings in many states, including some county courthouses. For example, a new courthouse and a federal building were erected for Richland County, and the old federal courthouse at 1737 Main Street in Columbia was renovated into city hall. Katherine Hammond, who was admitted to the bar in 1932, was an attorney on the Columbia staff of the Work Progress Administration.

The Social Security Act provided retirement, unemployment, and certain welfare benefits for those unable to work. The practice of law in the Social Security Administration became another legal specialty available to women attorneys. Thomasine G. Mason, included in this study, became the chief judge of South Carolina's Social Security Office of Hearing and Appeals.

When Roosevelt ran for re-election in 1936, South Carolina cast ninety-eight percent of its votes for him. "Oh, Roosevelt's picture was everywhere, in every law office," said T. Allen Legare, who became an attorney in 1941. "It was right there where the clients could see it beside the Bible and the picture of Lincoln and his dictum 'A lawyer's time and advice is his stock in trade.'" On the state level, an important piece of New Deal legislation was the passage of the Worker's Compensation Act in 1935. This law provided a forum for strict liability requiring employers, regardless of fault, to compensate employees for injuries arising out of and in the course of employment. Practice in that circumscribed area has led to a professional specialty. *Two* attorneys in this study have served as commissioners, and one has served as chairman of the Worker's Compensation Commission. Legislation passed to improve the national economy in the 1930s assuredly opened doors for legal specialties. Not to be overlooked, however, are two unrelated advances in South Carolina. A law school course in practice court taught in 1937 at the University of South Carolina was the only such course offered in any law school in the United States at that time. Columbia resident Judge Marcellus Whaley joined the faculty that year, teaching this subject into the 1950s. Judge Whaley called female students "Portia." He assigned all students, male and female, to a case in order for them to practice being a litigator. Judith Litman, nee Greenburg, was in the law class of 1940 and remembers that she participated in a trial in the course, as did her male colleagues.

The emancipation of women was further enhanced when in 1938, the South Carolina Supreme Court was asked to abrogate the legal fiction of the oneness of husband and wife in the case of *Bryant v. Smith,* et ux, 187 SC 448, 198 S.E. 20 (1938). This challenge was based on the 1925 act giving married women larger liberties with a balance of responsibilities. The act was then Section 400 of the code. The facts of this case arose at the General Reunion of the United Confederate Veterans in 1937, the issue being the election of a commander in chief. South Carolina delegates had voted for the defeated candidate. A motion was made and voted on to "throw out" the vote of the South Carolina delegation. According to the written opinion of the Supreme Court, while the vote was being taken, a husband called out, "Make them sit down. They are voting against us." His wife then rushed over to the plaintiff and struck him in the face, "shocking and dazing him and knocking his glasses to the floor," for which he claimed three thousand dollars in damages. At issue was the common law of a husband's liability for the acts of his wife. The husband of Minnie Holman (who was admitted to the bar in 1918) was the judge in the lower level court, and he upheld the common law. Attorney for the appellant was C. T. Graydon, father of Sarah Graydon (who was admitted to the bar in 1944). In its decision, the court noted that the Legislature had taken successive steps in the direction of repealing the servitude of marriage and found that the common law was nullified by the 1925 statute.

A court decision reinforcing the independence of women in South Carolina was a highlight in an otherwise lackluster decade for female advancement. The following biographies will show that eight of the fourteen new Portias of the 1930s studied law in a private office to prepare for the bar examination. None of the eight became trial lawyers. Some of the women who attended law school during this period did not take personal responsibility for their decision, saying they went to law school because it was their father's goal for them or they found themselves in law school by "happenstance." Only one, Mildred Huggins, had the expectation of becoming a litigator, and she succeeded.

The repercussions of the Great Depression did not fully dissipate until World War II. The harsh economy certainly affected the expectations of all new attorneys. Several of them had no noteworthy career until well after this decade. The 1930s was a time when circumstances tended to overwhelm resolution.

(18) Hannah R. Axelman
admitted December 18, 1931
1902–1959

"I could not believe the nerve of her, to be an attorney," sniffed one member of the synagogue about the rabbi's wife who became the first woman lawyer in Charleston. Fifty years later, the Historic Charleston Foundation had Hannah Axelman's portrait painted and hung in the then newly restored 1792 Charleston County Courthouse, a building venerated for its judicial and historical significance.

Axelman, nee Rubinrott, graduated from New York University Law School in 1923 before her marriage. After her graduation, she served as a law clerk for an attorney in private practice, a step necessary to qualify for the New York Bar. In 1926, she married Rabbi Benjamin G. Axelman, who had attended night school at Fordham University Law School in the Bronx, New York. He would remark that he had also wanted to be a lawyer, "so I married one." The year they married, the Axelmans came to Charleston, where he served the orthodox congregation of B'rith Shalom, and Beth Israel, as well as being principal of the Hebrew School.

Three prominent members of the local bar certified to the Supreme Court as to Axelman's fitness to take the South Carolina Bar examination. After admission to the bar, she hung a sign on the outside of her house, "Hannah R. Axelman, Attorney at Law." Her son, Judge Joseph Axelman of Virginia, remembers his mother receiving some legal fees paid in vegetables. He also says the city's mayor frequently appointed her to serve on various committees as the "token woman."

Charleston County Probate Judge (ret.) Gus H. Pearlman remembers that he and Karl Karesh, on at least two occasions when they were teenagers, went to the court of common pleas in order to hear Axelman argue in the courtroom. One reason Judge Pearlman says he was attracted to her was because she had big breasts ". . . but you have to remember—I was fifteen years old." During the 1930s, oratory was a required subject at the high school in Charleston where Axelman gave pro bono tutorial lessons in public speaking to the teenagers. She made young Jack Brickman, now a lawyer, be the try-out audience.

Axelman's personal behavior was subject to the laws of the orthodox Jewish faith. She could not shake a man's hand because men are not allowed to touch a married woman. As a married woman, she wore a hat in public since religious rules required her to conceal her hair from all men except her husband. Additionally, she could not practice law on Saturday, her Sabbath.

The Axelmans moved to Baltimore in 1943, where Rabbi Axelman served another synagogue. Although the Maryland

Supreme Court customarily heard motions for admission only on Saturday mornings, the court granted an exception for Axelman to be heard on a Friday. After her admission there, she continued in the practice of law.

Not only did she have "the nerve" to be a lawyer, but she was also a redhead and a Yankee.

(19) Leah Townsend
admitted June 17, 1932
1888–1981

"A woman lawyer at the beginning of the Great Depression with scarcely the courage of a mouse in the clash of competition was a natural for an office lawyer; one who spends their life with small victories and slight errors," said Leah Townsend. With what Townsend described as the "old method," she studied law in the office of her half brother, Peter H. McEachin, on West Evans Avenue in Florence. Townsend was admitted to the bar in June 1932, and the firm became McEachin and Townsend. The two of them were scions of a South Carolina family of lawyers that spans six generations. Townsend took her undergraduate degree from Winthrop and a doctor of philosophy from the University of South Carolina, where her history dissertation was titled *South Carolina Baptists 1670–1805*—a book still in print.

At one time, she said the only prejudice she experienced in the law office was from some of the firm's clients who refused to discuss their business with a woman. However, at an earlier date, she was quoted as saying that one reason for her acceptance in the town was because "I have *never* tried a case in Florence itself." Locally, she was often known as Dr. Leah, a title referring to her doctor of philosophy. "It has always seemed to me that both judges and jury have some slight feeling of prejudice against women lawyers in open court. This observation comes from the fact that it is unusual to see a woman in court rather than an actual prejudice." Dr. Leah emphatically felt that "a woman attorney will have no great opposition and will get just where her brain will take her." E. N. Zeigler, Esquire, her nephew and law partner, believes that she was aware of the fact that she had a scholarly, reticent nature. Her personality was not like that of the "flamboyant legal trial attorneys that I remember from my youth and early practice in Florence," he says. "Throughout her professional life, she was paid a net salary. Townsend felt that since she did not appear in court, it was more appropriate for her to be a paid employee rather than sharing in the profits of the law firm." Townsend remained in her practice until the age of eighty-three.

(20) Beatrice B. Free
admitted December 14, 1932
1901–1984

Beatrice Buchanan Free, better known as Bebe, was the first woman attorney in Greenwood County (more special even than Greenwood's famous white squirrels). Free hung out her lawyer's shingle at a piano store on South Main Street of Greenwood, where she was a secretary to the storeowner, John A. Holland. Holland, who was blind, had Free read to him all the books offered by the LaSalle Correspondence School of Law. Holland then failed the bar exam. Although Free passed, she continued as his secretary. Free's formal education was acquired in high school and at the Greenwood College of Commerce. Her son, H. B. "Buck" Free, wrote a description of her law practice, a document not dated and privately printed, *The Bebe Story: The Life and Times of Beatrice Buchanan Free.*

> She decided that she did not want to enter into any trial law or courtroom work, but she did want to be active in the legal field. She opened an office in Mr. Holland's building and hung out her shingle. She confined her early activities to drawing up legal papers, wills, handling estates, et cetera. She also began work with Kennedy, Kennedy, and Yow, a law firm in Augusta, Georgia, in arranging for a divorce for South Carolina residents. At the time, divorce was illegal in South Carolina. In order to meet this requirement, one of the divorcing spouses would have to establish residence in Augusta. She was never totally sure that this was 'right' and often worried about it, eventually giving it up.

As I look back now, this was probably very profitable for her. This was in the early to middle thirties, and the country was still in the throes of the great depression. She later stated to me that she never took the case if a divorce was to be contested and that, to the best of her memory, she helped in about thirteen total cases.

Sometime during the Great Depression, Holland filed for bankruptcy and later filed a reorganization plan. In the interim, Free and Holland's other employees worked without pay. After Holland's death, Free became a full-time employee at the South Main Street Baptist Church. Her son remembers her personality as "always upbeat." He also recalls seeing her drive sixty miles an hour down Greenwood's South Main Street, evidence of her exuberance.

(21) Katharine F. Hammond
admitted December 14, 1932
1909–1993

Katharine Hammond used her legal education to augment her business responsibilities as manager of a family plantation, Silver Bluff, in Aiken County. Also, from time to time, she appeared in criminal court with the defendant on behalf of one of her employees. These occurrences were after she had been left a widow with three small children. Her great-grandfather had acquired Silver Bluff and the adjacent plantation, Kathwood, in the 1830s. Harry Suber, one of her sons, says, "I can remember her commenting that in business dealings with men, women were not taken seriously. I know of only one instance of her filing a formal legal brief. It involved a claim for damages for ships lost in the War of 1812 belonging to her great-great-grandfather, Christopher C. Fitzsimons of Charleston."

After receiving a bachelor of law degree from National University in Washington, D.C., by attending night school, Hammond frequently told the story that her Uncle Henry (Judge Henry Cumming Hammond of Augusta, Georgia) challenged her to study law and promised to pay her tuition if she would. It is noteworthy that her older sister was one of the first women to receive a degree from the Medical School of Georgia. Their grandfather had degrees in both medicine and law. Their great-grandfather, James Henry Hammond, was also a lawyer and subsequently a governor of South Carolina, as well as a United States senator.

When Hammond signed the South Carolina Supreme Court's book of enrollment, she designated Kathwood, the plantation where she lived most of her life, as her hometown. In the *Columbia City Directory* for 1936, Katharine Hammond is identified as having a position with the United States Works Progress Administration, with a residence at 514 Congaree Street. That same year, she married James Calvin Suber, a Clemson engineer.

Harry Suber says, "I was always proud that my mother was a member of the bar. When I was younger, I was disappointed that she didn't practice, but as I grew older, I was grateful that she decided that her first priority was that of mother."

(22) F. Mildred Huggins
admitted June 13, 1933
1909–1972

Mildred Huggins engaged in a successful full-service, solo law practice throughout her career, with a caseload that included defending felony criminal cases. She was admitted to the bar on the diploma privilege after graduation from the University of South Carolina Law School. To help her start a practice, her father built her a law office building next door to the police court on Main Street in Timmonsville, Florence County. Huggins was then only one of two lawyers in town. Her family knew everyone in Timmonsville, where her father was a businessman, elected official, and farmer. Huggins's sisters called her a "kitchen lawyer" because so many of her African-American clients came to their kitchen door for a consultation.

In 1958, the *Florence Morning News* quoted Huggins as having said, "The most interesting cases in my practice were in the local police and magistrate courts, and for me, it was practically a daily occurrence." E. M. Floyd, a Darlington County attorney, gives her credit for being the first local lawyer to make tape recordings of the proceedings in a magistrate's court prior to those courts actually having recording devices. Floyd remembered that Huggins said the presence of the tape machine had an effect on the testimony. "For the first decade after I opened offices, I enjoyed a great practice here," she told the *Florence Morning News*. "Since then, over a dozen local boys have become lawyers and settled here."

United States Senator Strom Thurmond told me on September 30, 1999, "Her family was among my friends. Her father was in the Legislature. I had an opportunity to size her up pretty good, and she was an able lawyer and dependable in advising on legal matters."

Even before her undergraduate days at Winthrop College, Huggins was intrigued by the practice of the only two lawyers in Timmonsville at that time, as well as her father's political activities. She often denied that she had encountered any opposition from male lawyers in her courthouse experience. However, her contemporary, Leah Townsend, the other Florence County female attorney, once declared that courtroom lawyers were "mean" to Mildred at first, but later resistance ceased. In 1949, Governor Strom Thurmond appointed Huggins to a state commission to propose revisions to the state constitution. Mid-career, she served as president of a statewide organization known as The Council for the Common Good, an association of all the major women's groups in the state. The Council for the Common Good worked to remove the exemption of women from jury service. South Carolina women, however, were not drawn for the jury pool until 1967, just five years before Huggins retired from her law practice.

(23) Celia Keels Black
admitted June 13, 1933
1910–1982

As a second-year law student in 1933, Celia Black passed the bar examination and was admitted to the practice; however, she continued with her legal education until graduation. Black claimed to have gone to law school only because it was her father's desire, although he was not an attorney. Black's daughter, Mary Helen Spadlin, recalls her mother telling about being excused from the

criminal law classroom when the professor and students were studying the subject of rape.

Black never practiced law, but she clerked for a lawyer and knew
that she was paid less than a man. She rationalized, "Males have families to feed." Later, Black owned and operated a gift shop at Five
Points Shopping Plaza in Columbia. Black named it "Moore's Gift
Shop" in recognition of her husband, J. D. Moore. She served as president of the Five Points Merchants Association and made other civic
contributions. Spadlin says that sometime in the 1970s, after the feminist movement of the 1960s, Black came to the conclusion that
early on in her life, she had felt pressure not to succeed as a woman
lawyer.

(24) Mary Stewart Allan
admitted October 14, 1933
1908–1975

After Mary Allan graduated from the College of Charleston in
1928, she became what is known locally as "a Broad Street secretary,"
a colloquialism describing a secretary employed in an office on the
Charleston street where most of the law offices were located. Allan
worked in the office of Hyde, Mann, and Figg as secretary to Robert
Figg. Each day, she would study law in his library while waiting for
Figg to come to the office. Allan never told Figg that she was reading law. One day in 1933, she and her mother drove their car to
Columbia, where Allan took and passed the bar examination. She
did not return to Figg's office as his secretary. Mary Allan was no
stranger to women pioneering in the professions. Her aunt, Sarah
Campbell Allan, became the first woman to be licensed as a medical
doctor in South Carolina, in 1895.

Later in the 1930s, Allan completed a master's degree program
in social work at the University of Chicago, and then trained at the
Georgetown Visitation Convent in Washington, D.C. "Mary really
wanted to be a social worker," recalls her friend, Caroline Triest. "Her
goal had been to be a social worker in the South Carolina Prison
System, but she could not get the position." Her sister, Eleanor Allan

Hanson, says, "She believed she was not hired in that capacity because she was a female." Allan probably used her professional education as a volunteer social worker throughout much of the Great Depression. Her family could have supported her financially in this interest. Her family has owned the James M. Allan Jewelers of Charleston since 1855, and around 1945, Mary Allan became its manager.

In 1949, Allan organized Charleston's first Legal Aid Society. She accomplished this by soliciting the support of the president and members of the local bar and the Reverend Emmet M. Walsh, Catholic bishop, who was also chairman of the Legal Aid Division of the National Catholic Welfare Conference in Washington, D.C. The first office of this society was in the basement of Our Lady of Mercy Catholic Church at 79 America Street. Allan maintained office hours from 5 P.M. to 8 P.M. Monday through Friday. Five members of the local bar served as the society's board of advisors. The first year of operation, the society served ninety-six applicants. The following year, it moved to quarters at 33 Broad Street and had office hours from 9 A.M. to 1 P.M. six days a week. The local bar association paid the society's rent, utilities, and a small salary for Allan. Its 1957 Annual Report stated that the agency had served 638 cases, which included 622 new applications. The greatest demand was for financial support from the society. As her sister noted, "I remember at the dinner table she always had some tale of woe to tell us. She tried to teach people to budget their money so that they wouldn't get in the hands of usurers." I was Allan's substitute once while she was on vacation and was instructed by Allan not to recognize any attempt to break a marriage vow because she did not believe in divorce. Eventually, the United Fund supplied the budget requests for the society.

After twenty-two years of service, on July 30, 1970, the society closed due to lack of support from the United Fund Board, which determined that the Legal Aid Society services duplicated those of the federally financed Neighborhood Legal Association. Allan's salary for the last fiscal year was $7,500 out of the agency's budget of

$11,411. For several years prior to the agency closing, Allan had been trying to retire, but the board had persuaded her to remain.

(25) Elizabeth F. Eldridge
admitted December 16, 1933
1895–1975

In 1915, Elizabeth Eldridge, known as "Bet," the daughter of a Presbyterian minister, graduated from the University of Kentucky with a bachelor of arts degree. Two years later, she received a master's degree in English. She moved to Columbia the following year. However, it was not until 1919 that she took a position as secretary to Attorney Frank Thompkins of Columbia and began her professional career.

Fourteen years after her employment with Thompkins, Eldridge passed the bar examination and was admitted to the practice of law. Thompkins later formed a partnership association with John Gregg McMaster, who then became professionally associated with Eldridge for the balance of her career. He recalls that she occupied "second chair" to Thompkins in the trial of cases. "That partnership was basically a corporate firm. They represented Norfolk Southern Railway and through the years, there has been a lot of railway litigation," says Chief Justice (ret.) Bruce Littlejohn.

United States Senator Strom Thurmond recalls that she was a very capable person. He says Thompkins was performing a magnificent service. He observed, "She prepared the work, and he tried the cases."

(26) Sarah Smarr Calhoun
admitted June 4, 1935
1912–1991

Sarah Calhoun of Georgetown was not only an attorney, but she was also a baroness and a Converse College alumna. A classmate of hers at the university law school, Sarah Glymph, says, "Sarah made it clear at all times that she was at law school only because her father wanted her to be there, and that she did not intend to be a lawyer.

Nevertheless, she was a good student and was well-liked." Calhoun's father, not a lawyer himself, but a railway agent, evidently had high aspirations for his daughter. His sister was married to South Carolina Circuit Court Judge Thomas Sease of Spartanburg. Chief Justice (ret.) Bruce Littlejohn believes that Calhoun became Judge Sease's court reporter. However, her cousin, Mary Ann Lockhart, believes that Calhoun was a court reporter for United States District Judge C. C. Wyche.

The undisputed fact in the life of Sarah Calhoun is her chance meeting of Baron Louis Montant at Spartanburg's United States Army Camp Croft. Upon their marriage, Sarah Montant became a baroness. Professionally, the baron was a research scientist. His inherited title was of Italian origin. The couple lived most of their married life in Cincinnati, where she was not active in the legal profession. Upon his retirement, they moved to Georgetown. Ralph M. Ford, personal representative to her estate, says, "In a dispute, Sarah always told us she was right because she was a lawyer. She did like to brag a little, but we were all amazed to find out that she was a baroness. Louis's mother saw to it that they were always in the *Social Register of New York*."

(27) Mary Polhemus
admitted December 9, 1935
1894–1951

While a few women were becoming members of the South Carolina Bar in the 1920s, Mary Polhemus, known by her friends and family as May, was daily peddling her bicycle from her home at 56 Smith Street to Broad Street in Charleston. She was what was then known as a "typewriter" in the law office of J. D. E. Meyer. Sometime during the 1920s, she acquired the shorthand skills of a court reporter. In the 1930s, newly elected United States Senator James F. Byrnes asked her to work in his Washington office. She agreed, provided she could leave if she did not like Washington. She was back in Meyer's office in a few months.

Meyer, known to the bar as "Major Meyer," said to her, "May, you know so much about the law, you could pass the examination." In 1935, she did just that and was admitted to the bar. Niece, Mary Jo Ross, recalls seeing Polhemus consulting with personal clients in their front parlor. Ross says her aunt loved being an attorney. "It was her be-all and end-all." Polhemus was associated with Meyer, a leading criminal trial attorney, for thirty-five years.

Meyer was the financial benefactor of his three Hollings nephews. As each completed his college education, Polhemus prepared an office for him. The oldest, Robert, a Harvard-educated lawyer, remembered that Polhemus signed some pleadings for the firm. The youngest is now United States Senator Ernest F. Hollings. Senator Hollings was especially fond of Polhemus, saying, "She was so legal in her mind, that when Meyer imported himself a German bride, Polhemus asked, 'Do you think they will have issue?'"

After the death of Polhemus in 1951, Meyer had a new brass plate erected on the outside of the firm's building that read, "Mary Polhemus, Attorney at Law."

(28) Sarah Glymph
admitted June 2, 1936
1912–

When Sarah Glymph of Pomaria, Newberry County, graduated from law school at the University of South Carolina in 1936, she was by no means committed to the profession. From her present home in Virginia, she wrote in 1999, "I became a lawyer by happenstance. Actually, I expected to get married and have six children. For me, law was then a temporary thing, but it turned out to be my whole life. I arrived at law school with no ambition to become a lawyer, and having no conception of what I was undertaking." Nevertheless, in her undergraduate days at Winthrop, she was president of the Debaters League and a speaker at commencement. Later, she was elected president of the Law Students Federation.

After Glymph's first year in law school, she took a job checking real estate titles for the law office of her property professor, a position she held during the last two years of law school, and continued for six months after graduation. This professor then recommended Glymph for her next two professional positions, checking and clearing property titles in Chesterfield County and as a research assistant to a Columbia University professor and author of texts on a creditor's rights and remedies. Glymph had such confidence in her professor's judgment that she did not even discuss salary before taking a position. "I did not go through that frayed cuff period," Glymph says in referring to the experience of her classmate, Bruce Littlejohn, as described in his autobiography published by the South Carolina Bar Foundation in 1987, *Littlejohn's Half Century at the Bench and Bar (1936–1986).*

Littlejohn notes on pages 17-18, "During my first year at the practice, I recall seeing a lawyer trying a case in the Spartanburg County Courthouse with a patch on the seat of his britches." Littlejohn took a desk in another lawyer's office with the understanding that fees would not be shared, but he could provide some professional services in lieu of contributing to the eight dollars a month rent. The secretary earned fifteen dollars a month. Glymph's marriage to Richard William Wilcox, and the ensuing children, took her out of the work force until the post World War II era. For a short time in 1947, she was the law school librarian and then an executive secretary to a South Carolina congressman. After Harry Truman was elected president, she accepted a position in the Commercial Litigation Division of the Department of Justice, embarking on a thirty-year career as a federal attorney. The acme of her professional life was her work in the Civil Division. She says:

> *Of all my jobs, I enjoyed that one the most. I was fortunate enough to have served under and with excellent lawyers. Once a matter was referred to the Justice Department for litigation, the department alone had exclusive responsibility for the conduct of the litigation including compromising. I never took the responsibility lightly.*
>
> *Perhaps the most important cases that I handled were those involving failed tax shelter HUD projects, certainly from a money standpoint they were. Around the mid-1970s the Department of*

Housing and Urban Development (HUD) referred cases resulting from defaulted loans on HUD-insured projects, and most of these cases were assigned to me. These are projects of various kinds in which high-income individuals had invested in order to eliminate or reduce their taxes through use of tax preferences known as tax shelters. The success or failure of the projects was not of paramount interest, and these projects failed by the hundreds across the country. In a status report on my HUD cases made June 1976, I listed my 128 HUD cases and the amount of money involved in each, totaling $329,284,892.97—about one-third of a billion dollars.

A small group of cases, about fifteen or twenty a year, which added a little human interest to my work, involved bequests and gifts to the United States and they added spice to my business-type cases. Some of the things bequeathed were copies of the Declaration of Independence and the Gettysburg Address in Lincoln's handwriting, art, collections of various nature, and many more, including an old villa in Italy.

It was only in the last six or seven years before Glymph retired in 1978 that she served with other women lawyers in the Justice Department.

(29) Grace A. White
admitted December 19, 1936
1910–

During a Beaufort County High School debate judged by Attorney Brantley Harvey, Sr. in the late 1920s, Grace White made a career decision. She, too, would be an attorney—a decision she has carried through with great éclat during her long life.

This Marine Corps "brat" became the first tax attorney in South Carolina, the first woman attorney in Beaufort County, and she is now the senior member of the Beaufort County Bar. "My dad raised me according to Marine Corps regulations, and I always wanted to know the reasons for the regulations. Probably, this unconsciously pointed me in the direction of being an attorney."

White entered a six-year curriculum at George Washington University that led to a bachelor's and law degree. During the time she was in the law school program, White was the only woman in her day-time law classes. "I conducted myself in a manner to show that I didn't expect any special consideration and that I was not trespassing." White was admitted to the District of Columbia Bar in 1936 and tried, but failed, to get a job in the Justice Department.

They needed another lawyer in the Justice Department like they needed a hole in the head. By that time, my parents had retired to a home in the historic section of Beaufort and prevailed upon me to join them. After I was admitted to the bar in this state, I became the eighth lawyer in Beaufort County. I volunteered to 'polish a chair' at the law office of William 'Bill' Elliott, a member of the South Carolina House of Representatives, who was then closing his office three days each week when he had to be in Columbia. He was his own secretary. My expectations were that I could be successful enough to buy a house on the river.

I started doing income tax returns because no one else wanted to do them, and income taxes were becoming a part of everyone's life. I was making two bucks a pop in that first year. The instructions for the 1040 tax forms were on four pages; now, they are twelve to fifteen volumes. W-2 income tax forms were first issued in 1943. When the military draft was instituted at the beginning of World War II, an eight-page questionnaire was mailed to all possible draftees and the bar was asked to assist them in completing the form pro bono. Soon, I got so I could just look at someone coming through the door and I could tell whether or not they were a paying client.

At first, Elliott would not take any rent, so I bought some office supplies and finally I made him take some rent. It was during this time when I had my first experience with title abstracting. Elliott and I abstracted the title and conducted the closing transaction for the sale of Bray's Island to F. B. White, president of U.S. Tire and Rubber Company. This was about the beginning when rich Yankees began moving down here and buying plantations. F. B. White used it as a tax shelter by turning it into a chicken and dairy farm. The farm sold milk and eggs commercially. Today, Bray's Island is quite a large residential development.

Representing tax clients led to probate estate work and estate tax returns. After about ten years of this office arrangement, Elliott became a magistrate and needed more space. I then opened my own office across Bay Street at 907. Brantley Harvey, Sr. pushed some real estate title work my way, an act that I appreciated. Eventually, I applied and was granted permission to practice before the Internal Revenue Service. The very next year after I was accepted, their rules changed to require annual approval of attorneys, certified public accountants, and Internal Revenue agents.

White had been "grandmothered" in and never had to apply again. By the 1950s and 1960s, White says she was serving maybe one hundred fifty tax clients and was filing some five hundred returns annually.

Other Beaufort lawyers began to do tax returns because they found out how lucrative it was. I probably represented the Pruitt family over a longer period of time than any other; they were my oldest clients. They were my clients from 1938 to 1993. I did their annual returns and I handled four of the family estates. The father, Ed Pruitt, ran a typical neighborhood store and he could justify every expense or payment. The Internal Revenue Service never audited him, and he had a big estate. At his death, he owned nineteen parcels of real property.

In 1978, White began to experience the onset of macular degeneration of the retina, which eventually caused her to move her law office to her home, where she still does her own tax returns. White also continues to pay her bar association dues and her City of Beaufort business license. "I don't want to give up my status as senior member of the Beaufort Bar."

(30) Myrtle Johnson
admitted June 18, 1937
1902–1981

"If ever there was an organized person in this world, it was the late Mrs. Myrtle Jeffords. I'm firmly convinced that she took the pearly gates by storm." This quote, taken from the *Darlington News and Press* on February 5, 1981, is from a column written by Dwight Dana on the occasion of Myrtle Johnson Jefford's death. Johnson's classroom education was in the public schools and the Massey Business College of Richmond, Virginia. She started her first job in 1919 at the Darlington Roller Mills when she was seventeen years old. Johnson's professional career began in the law office of Dargan and Paulling, where she was a secretary to George E. Dargan. While associated with Dargan, she studied law, passed the bar examination, and was admitted to the bar in 1937. Johnson's marriage to Otto Calhoun Jeffords in 1940 took her out of the legal profession. After his death eight years later, she accepted a position as secretary in the office of Senator J. P. Mozingo, also an attorney. After three years with Mozingo, she became the secretary of Darlington County Solicitor Robert L. Kilgo. In 1956, Johnson announced that she was a candidate for the state Legislature, the first woman in that county to run for public office. Eventually, she withdrew from the political race due to the "press of work." The apogee of Johnson's professional career was in serving as secretary and treasurer of the City of Darlington for nearly a decade, the first woman to hold that position. Simultaneously, she served as secretary and treasurer of the Darlington County Bar Association.

(31) Mary Grace Andrishok
admitted June 17, 1938
1906–1993

> *Bank failures, suicides, and bankruptcies were all about, but one day, all the banks in the nation closed. There was no money! I remember how serious it was—no jobs! Men were losing jobs (of which my husband was one) and people were trying to live from day to day. Men needed jobs for their sanity as well as their homes. I learned that one should take every opportunity to prepare oneself for a place in the work force. About that time, I went to work in a law office, studied day and night for about three and a half years, took the South Carolina Bar examination, and was admitted to the South Carolina Bar.*

As the Great Depression was drawing to a close in 1938, Mary Grace Andrishok was completing her law studies in the office of Joel I. Allen of Mullins, a solo practitioner who had an office up a flight of stairs off Main Street. Born in 1906 in Latta, Andrishok grew up in Mullins. After several years as a student at Winthrop College, she left to get married in 1926. Although her husband's job was terminated during the Depression, Andrishok continued in the law practice with Allen until about 1950. "I believe Aunt Mary Grace did try several cases in the courtroom," says H. E. Ulmer, her nephew. "She was a 'take charge person.' If she was involved in the situation, no doubt was left as to whom would initiate action to achieve proper results."

After her husband died in 1949, Andrishok accepted a position as administrator of a sixty-bed private hospital owned by James L. Martin, M.D. Her law license was then displayed in the office of the Martin Hospital. Andrishok claimed her legal knowledge served her well in the health care field, and she continued in this work until her retirement. "After the hospital closed, she occasionally did legal-financial work for the various firms in the Mullins-Marion area until her death on October 27, 1993," Ulmer recalled.

The initial feminist impetus of South Carolina women seeking admission and acceptance at the bar did not survive the exigencies of the Great Depression intact. Aspirations faded. The umbrella issue of women being excluded from jury service did not arouse Portias in the 1930s. The harshness of the economy thwarted pioneering spirit. Each of these women, however, displayed remarkable enterprise by studying law and being admitted to the bar. Given the social and economic circumstances, this was no small feat.

Hannah Rubinrott Axelman and
Rabbi Benjamin G. Axelman, in 1926.

Leah Townsend, 1932.   *Beatrice B. Free, 1932.*

F. Mildred Huggins, 1933.

Celia Keels Black, 1933.

Sarah Smarr Calhoun, 1935.

Mary Polhemus, 1935.

Sarah Glymph, 1936.

Grace A. White, 1936.

Mary Grace Andrishok, 1938.

South Carolina Law School Class of 1936.
Sarah Glymph on second row.

~ *Four* ~

"Fair Portia" Rides the Tide of Change

As the New Deal was gradually easing the United States' economy out of the Great Depression, Nazi Germany was stridently preparing for war. In 1938 and 1939, Adolf Hitler commenced aggression, seizing neighboring territory and nations, eventually drawing most of Europe into conflict. Japanese warmongering increased in the Far East. The United States maintained quasi-neutrality until December 7, 1941, when the Japanese bombed Pearl Harbor. Shortly thereafter, the United States was at war on two fronts.

Anticipation of war had already reduced the male population in schools of higher learning. Congress enacted the Selective Service System, recalled National Reserve officers, and activated the National Guard, moves that decimated the student body at all-male and co-ed colleges and universities.

Sarah Leverette, admitted in 1943, says that in her class, there was a rumor that the law school would have been closed if it had not been for the enrollment of the women students. The rumor may have been true, because when enrollment was at its lowest ebb, the president did not reveal to the trustees the law school ratio between male and female.

The following statistical student information was taken from each annual report of the president of the university to the board of trustees:

Year	Law School Students	Male	Female
1941	95	88	7
1942	49	42	7
1943	27	(data unavailable)	
1944	28	(data unavailable)	
1945	115	108	7

There were probably less than twenty women actually practicing law in South Carolina at the beginning of World War II. One of these, Alice Robinson (1929) of Columbia, is credited with holding together her law firm of Robinson and Robinson while the other partners were in the military, as noted in a previous chapter.

Although James F. Byrnes, a United States senator from South Carolina, was nominated to the U.S. Supreme Court in January 1942 by President Roosevelt, the overwhelming pressures of war were such that he resigned the following year to become director of war mobilization. The Selective Service, enacted before U.S. entry into the war, created such a tremendous labor shortage that the War Department encouraged women to go to work in offices and factories. Six million women took their first jobs between 1940 and 1941. The number of women in the labor force during this period rose from twenty-five to fifty-seven percent.

In 1943, the Women's Army Auxiliary Corps was given full military status. A 1933 Iowa law school graduate, Phyllis L. Propp, a WAAC, initiated the idea for women to serve in the Judge Advocate General's Corps and was its first member. While no lawyers in this present study joined the corps, there have been JAG women officers assigned to Fort Jackson Army Base in Columbia and probably at other military bases in the state. The military draft forced many men, with little advance notice, to arrange or rearrange their personal legal affairs. In order to provide some measure of protection for them, Congress passed an act protecting persons in the armed forces from certain civil proceedings by giving them a stay of court-ordered appearance. Specifically, the act included evictions, mortgages, leases, insurance payments, taxes, and domestic relations. Moreover, many newly inducted personnel needed a will and power-of-attorney documents. These young men created a boom in the need for legal counsel.

The war so consumed the legal profession in 1945 that the State Bar Association did not even conduct its annual meeting. However, later that same year, Germany and Japan conceded defeat. The imperatives of World War II had a distinctive effect on all women lawyers in this state. It was a time when there was a large transitory population. Seven of the eighteen women admitted to the bar in the first half of this decade resided only temporarily in this state. Two women who were permanent residents chose to spend their whole career with a federal agency. The unique circumstances facing new women attorneys during the war years places them in a category apart from those admitted to the bar between 1946 and 1950. For that reason, this chapter is divided into two sections, the first discussing the women admitted to the bar immediately, prior to, and during the war years; the latter eleven women were admitted postwar, when attitudes toward and expectations of women shifted dramatically.

(32) Judith Greenberg
admitted June 4, 1940

During the spring semester of her junior year at the University of South Carolina, Judith Greenberg started thinking about going to law school because her friends, Rembert Dennis and Julius "Bubba" Ness, were going to enroll. At that time, the university had a policy allowing students to substitute their first year in law school for their last one in the undergraduate academic program. Since Greenberg's grades were good, she decided to enter law school with her friends.

Not until her third year in law school, however, did she realize that she really had found her chosen profession.

Two weeks after her graduation and admission to the bar in June 1940, Greenberg married Samuel Litman, an engineering graduate student. "I think my expectations at graduation were to join a law firm and concentrate on property law. None of this happened because no law firm to which I applied gave me the opportunity to join them. Remember, this was 1940 in South Carolina—no women on the jury, no divorce, no place for women in the law." During the war years, the couple centered their life on achieving his doctorate and rearing two daughters. Judith retained her membership in the state bar while doing legal work for her family's Florence-based scrap metal business. She drew the necessary leases, formed a real estate partnership of Greenberg and Litman, and participated in real estate development and loan closings.

While Greenberg's daughters were growing up, she watched her friends, Dennis and Ness, who "were going great guns with their law degrees." Dennis had an iron grip on the state budget and Ness was headed for the state Supreme Court. After her husband died and the girls left home for college in the early 1970s, she felt dissatisfied with her life and asked a Columbia attorney, Kermit King, if she could work for him *gratis*. While associated with King, another lawyer, Frank Hartman, offered her a desk in his office. He needed her because he was frequently absent due to illness.

> *Soon, I became an experienced attorney. Frank died at the early age of thirty-two, and by his will, he left me his law practice. I learned fast that the monthly rent was one thousand dollars, the electric bill was about three hundred dollars, there was a payroll for two secretaries and a receptionist, and the lessee was liable for all repairs to the office. I was scared to death! I got one secretary a job at the synagogue, rented half the office to an architect, and offered Hartman's clients their files, but no one took them. Then, I closed out the files and gave his widow one-half the fees. Frank's practice included a lot of criminal work. The day after the funeral, a secretary handed me a file and told me I was due in criminal court. I almost had heart failure every time*

I went into that court and those cases worried me to death. The judges and all the other lawyers couldn't have been nicer; they were a help to me. I think I was one of the first to start getting public service for a criminal defendant. I held that office together for about a year. I have been full-time in the active practice ever since.

In 1981, I bought and remodeled a building at the corner of Calhoun and Lincoln Streets in Columbia, and I practiced law with my married name, Judith G. Litman. My architect tenant joined me in this move. My law practice now is limited to uncontested divorce and personal injury suits, and I close my office on Friday afternoons to go to the beauty shop.

Greenberg has remarried and practices as Judith Litman Lindau.

(33) Barbara Burt Brown
admitted December 13, 1940

Barbara Burt Brown was a resident of Spartanburg when she took the bar exam and was admitted to the bar in December 1940. Growing up in Alabama, she worked in her father's hotel and remembers the glimmer of aspiration when she heard guests making comments that she should be a lawyer when she grew up.

While she was a student at Vassar, Brown's father died. That loss, plus the lingering effects of the Great Depression, left the family with no money for graduate studies. Brown took a position with the United States Department of Agriculture in Washington and attended law school at night at George Washington University. Eventually, she was admitted to the District of Columbia Bar and married a Spartanburg native, Ben Hill Brown, Jr. While her husband was in military service during the war, she was an attorney in his father's Spartanburg law office. After the war, her husband was in the Foreign Service with the State Department. Between the 1960s and 1980s, they lived in Iraq, Libya, Turkey, Liberia, Indonesia, Kenya, and Tanzania.

In the olden days, State Department wives were not given the opportunity to work outside their home while stationed overseas.

However, while we were in Kenya, that tradition was broken and I joined the law firm of A. T. D. Ghadialy, Esquire, in Nyeri, Kenya. The practice was especially interesting in that country because it had two systems of law. One method was patterned after the British judicial standard and the other after African tribal law. I attended some seminars on the tribal law and found that it was based on common sense. I did not try any cases in court, but I did take some depositions from persons who were incarcerated and saw that their jails were far below American standards.

Confidentiality was, of course, honored, but I can relate the story of one Kenyan who sought a divorce from one of his wives. Affluent tribal Kenyans usually had more than one wife. His complaint stemmed from an event after a dance. He had told this wife that it was time to leave and they departed according to custom, she walking behind him. At some point, he no longer heard her footsteps following him and he retraced his steps to the dance where he found her continuing to enjoy the festivities. Sorry, I don't know how the case was finished.

When she returned to the states, Brown earned a master's degree in environmental law from George Washington University. She and Ben Brown, Jr. later divorced. He died in 1989. Remarried now to Burt Behrens, she is retired from the practice of law and lives in Pensacola, Florida.

(34) Emma Lee Crumpacker.
admitted December 30, 1940

Emma Lee Crumpacker was the first woman attorney in the city of Conway, as well as in the county of Horry. In 1937, she graduated from Duke University Law School and was admitted to the North Carolina Bar under her maiden name, Emma Lee Smith. She practiced law in Durham until she and her husband moved to Conway, where he had a position with the Canal Wood Corporation. At that time and since then, the company is one of the major timber corporations in the low country.

Three Conway attorneys endorsed Emma Crumpacker to the state Supreme Court—Rubin Long, Enoch S. C. Baker, and Lonnie C. Causey.

Apparently, Emma Crumpacker did not remain long in Conway nor establish a law practice. No records of her have been located in the county documents.

(35) Opal Kelly Hesse
admitted May 16, 1941
1901–1969

Opal Kelly Hesse was a member of the Illinois Bar when she took the oath in South Carolina in May 1941. She relocated to this state in February of that year after marrying a Charleston pharmacist, Ernest C. Hesse. Born Opal Eunice Kelly on January 13, 1901, Hesse would have been familiar with the first wave of feminism during the 1920s. It was during this period that she and a girlfriend undertook a great adventure for women of that day—they hitchhiked to California and back! In 1925, she graduated from Bradley University in Peoria, where she excelled in sports. Following that, she enrolled in law school at De Paul University in Chicago, where she helped to pay for her education by holding down a full-time job. After graduation, Hesse was admitted to the Illinois Bar on December 15, 1932, and joined her father's law firm, practicing under the name of Kelly and Kelly for a period of nine years. Hesse never practiced law after she moved to Charleston. I met Hesse on several occasions and know she considered joining a practice, but an arrangement never materialized.

(36) Myrtle Holcombe
admitted June 12, 1941

Myrtle Holcombe is cited in the *Columbia City Directory* as living with her parents, William R. and Ruth Holcombe, at 1414 Woodrow while she was a law student. Her father was identified as being a barber. In the years after admission to the bar, neither she nor her parents are listed in local directories. How, or if, she used her legal education is not known. The university's yearbook, *Garnet and Black* (1941), gives this information about Holcombe: "Baptist Student Union, Sec-Treas. of Freshman law class, Historian of Jr. and Sr. law class, A.B. Univ. of California at Los Angeles."

(37) Thomasine Grayson Mason
admitted June 2, 1941
1918–

> *My desire to become a lawyer happened one day when I was in the ninth grade and it never wavered. We were in Columbia and my brother was driving. Because in those days cars parked head-on along Main Street, other cars would illegally park behind them. In our case, we were parked head-on, and a woman illegally parked behind us, and then hit our car. Clearly, it was not my brother's fault, but she challenged my mother claiming she knew a lawyer and was 'going to get him.' My mother figured it was far more expensive to get a lawyer and travel to Columbia from our home in Summerton to appear in court than to just pay for the fender-bender. It was that exact moment when I decided that I would be a lawyer and no one was going to intimidate me like that. Lawyers became my heroes.*

During her second year in law school, Thomasine Grayson Mason passed the necessary examination and was admitted to the bar, but she remained in law school through graduation. In her third year, she served as chief justice of the scholastic fraternity, Wig and Robe. During World War II, Mason accepted a position as a Civil Service representative and was assigned to Atlanta, Athens, and the Charleston Navy Yard. She accepted this post after "no legal firm in Columbia would give me a chance. I even offered to work as a clerk or receptionist, but one firm told me that I would not be satisfied and would always want to go to court. They were right."

Subsequently, her father's ill health caused her to return to his one thousand-acre Clarendon County farm, cotton gin, grain elevator, seed cleaning, and treatment plant. The demands of this operation sent her back to a classroom to learn cotton classing. When her nephew was ready to take over the family business, Mason inquired about a refresher course in the law school. The dean advised her to volunteer to observe in a small law office, and she chose the firm of Richardson and James in Sumter. When these attorneys thought she was ready, Mason rented a little office in Manning and resolved to be there daily from nine to five whether she had a client or not. Within a year, she had developed an active practice. After three years, she closed her office and accepted a position as a trial attorney with the Department of Justice in its District of Columbia Civil Division and General Claims. In 1971, she became the chief federal administrative law judge of Social Security Hearing and Appeals. In addition, she sits on its Appeals Council as an active member.

Mason is one of the few women ever elected to the South Carolina Senate, and the first to be appointed to the prestigious Judiciary Committee, an appointment of great esteem to lawyers. Senator Mason represented Sumter and Clarendon Counties (1967–1968).

(38) Mrs. Sidney S. Gober
admitted June 13, 1941

According to the *County of Augusta City Directory* in 1940, Mrs. Sidney S. Gober was an office secretary for Isaac S. Peeples, Jr., a lawyer and Richmond County attorney. Her husband was William A. (Sidney) Gober, a news editor of the *Augusta Chronicle*, (who for some reason went by the name Sidney S. Gober). He is identified as "William A. (Sidney S.) Gober in the 1941 directory; she is cited as a lawyer in the office of Peeples, but neither she nor her husband are listed after that date. It is likely that Peeples had clients in both Georgia and South Carolina. World War II, a transitory period for many, may have taken the Gobers to another location.

(39) Cassandra E. Maxwell
admitted December 11, 1941
1910–1974

Cassandra Maxwell was born in Orangeburg in 1910, the daughter of John Maxwell and Katherine Louise Cardozo. Her paternal grandfather had been a state senator and chairman of its Education Committee. Her maternal great-grandfather, Francis Lewis Cardozo, was a graduate from law school at South Carolina College, now the University of South Carolina, in the class of 1876. She and United States Supreme Court Justice Benjamin N. Cardozo shared a common ancestor.

Maxwell made a unique and distinguished contribution to the history of women lawyers in South Carolina. She was the first woman to be given law school faculty status and the first African-American woman lawyer admitted to this bar.

C. Walker Limehouse, a member of the Orangeburg Bar, remembers Cassandra Maxwell as the daughter of successful grocery merchants, whose assortment of gourmet food attracted all the residents of Orangeburg. The family members were active communicants at St. Paul's Episcopal Church. Maxwell attended Spelman College in Atlanta and then enrolled at Howard University, where she received both a bachelor of arts degree and a bachelor of laws degree. In 1939, one of the formative years of the National Association for the Advancement of Colored People, she held her first position as secretary to Thurgood Marshall, then its chief attorney.

After her admission to the South Carolina Bar in December 1941, Maxwell opened a law office above the family grocery, which was located on Russell Street just off Railroad Corner. Limehouse says, "Cassandra Maxwell undertook some tough litigation and was successful with it. I followed her career with interest, and she and I exchanged information and pleasantries regularly. She had the respect of the bar."

In order to prevent African-American students from enrolling in the law school of the University of South Carolina, the state established a law school at South Carolina State College in Orangeburg in 1947. Maxwell was given faculty status, teaching courses in credit transactions, contracts, pleadings, and moot court training. Russell Brown and Newton W. Pough, former students at the Orangeburg law school, remember and admire her success of prevailing in cases to set aside a number of partition actions initiated by mortgagees who had taken a deed to property due to one late payment. In 1950, she married a biology professor, James H. Birnie. The couple moved to Atlanta, where she again established a law practice, and the couple was on the faculty of Moorehouse College. Maxwell participated in the developing years of the Civil Rights Movement by using her professional knowledge in the protection of residential rights.

When Maxwell's husband retired, they moved to Philadelphia. There she received the Republican nomination for a civil judgeship, but was not elected. She maintained active participation with the Republican Party, and President Nixon appointed her as a member of the Interim Board of Directors of the Student Loan Marketing Association. Maxwell died in 1974.

(40) Muriel E. McCay
admitted January 15, 1942

Muriel E. McCay and her husband, George, were sworn into the South Carolina Bar during the same ceremony. Both were graduates of George Washington University Law School. Muriel McCay's undergraduate studies were taken at the College of Charleston. George's sister, Margie McCay, believes the couple met the residential qualifications to take the South Carolina Bar exam because his father was a Charleston businessman, and at that time, they were expected to represent him.

The two McCay lawyers never opened a law office. All of their married life they resided on Chair Ridge Road in McLean, Virginia, where they established a real estate partnership, "McCay and McCay, Real Estate."

This partnership developed land known as Langley, now the most prestigious community in McLean. Both are deceased.

(41) Eva Bryan Wilson
admitted May 25, 1942

After Eva Bryan Wilson graduated from the University of South Carolina Law School and was admitted to the bar, she accepted a position as a junior attorney in the office of Price Administration in

Washington, D.C. A few years later, she became vice counsel for the Foreign Service of the State Department and took assignments in Brisbane, Sydney, Calcutta, and Paris. Her responsibilities included interviewing and making decisions about citizenship, passport applications, and birth, marriage, and death registrations. With regard to shipping and seamen, she was concerned with renewal and re-entry certificates, documentation as to export, and ultimate importations into the United States. Her office would code and decode messages from the State Department. "In some assignments, you only dealt with one subject such as citizenship, visas, et al. On other assignments, you had responsibility in several categories," she recalls.

Wilson resigned from the Foreign Service in 1952, when she married Christopher Cookson, an English national, and she was not thereafter employed in the legal profession. After her husband died, she continued to live for a time in Somerset County, England, where she was a volunteer for a local Citizens Advisory Bureau, which directed residents to sources that could provide them with information they were seeking. Currently, Cookson lives in her home county of Barnwell and has served as a volunteer guardian ad litem in the family court.

(42) Sarah Elizabeth Leverette
admitted May 31, 1943
1919–

In all likelihood, Sarah Leverette has had more influence over twentieth century legal writing in South Carolina than any other person. Sarah taught the course to every law student at the University of South Carolina for a quarter of the century. During those years (1947–1972), she was also the school librarian. "Teaching legal writing has given me more satisfaction than any of the other areas of my professional life, and it has given me many good stories to tell. I'm still enjoying it! They invite me back to class reunions," says Leverette.

"When Ron Motley was a law student, he put his books in a carrel that was to be shared, and when he left the carrel, he took the door knob with him! Then I thought to myself, 'That student is motivated,'" related Leverette. Charleston attorney Ronald L. Motley is now one of the ten wealthiest lawyers in the United States.

Before she graduated magna cum laude from the university's undergraduate school, Leverette debated whether to go to medical or law school. Since she preferred English to chemistry, she chose law.

"My father was an Anderson County magistrate, and I guess I just wanted to do whatever he did, even though he was no attorney. But, when I told my parents I wanted to go to law school, I had to convince them I really wanted to do it for me and that I was not just trying to please my father."

Leverette's first professional position was doing legal research for the South Carolina Department of Labor. Two years later, the law school dean asked her to return to be the librarian and teach the legal writing course, first sending her to Columbia University for post-graduate studies in legal research and law library administration.

When on December 31, 1971, Louise Wideman, admitted in 1945, retired as an industrial commissioner from the Workman's Compensation Commission, Governor John C. West appointed Leverette in her place. "In a way, this position was a continuation of my associations with students who were then in the practice of law. A Charleston attorney, Irving Steinberg, brought one interesting case and the issue centered around a school teacher who was injured while stepping down the interior stairs in her home and at the same time carrying school books preparatory to walking out the door to go to school. I awarded the teacher compensation, finding that the books were the approximate cause of the injury. The case was appealed to the Supreme Court and my opinion was upheld."

At the time of her retirement, Leverette was chairman of the Industrial Commissioners at the Workman's Compensation Commission. She then became licensed as a Realtor, and says, "My annual fees to maintain my Realtor's license are more expensive than the fees to maintain my law license."

(43) Edith Pratt Breeden
admitted June 28, 1944
1922–1997

". . . a fair Portia!" is how the South Carolina Supreme Court described Edith Pratt Breeden in *Schwartz v. Mount Vernon-Woodberry Mills, Inc.*, 206 SC 227; 33 S.E. (2) 517 (1945). To be given a complimentary personal appellation in a Supreme Court decision is an accolade for any member of the bar, and the court was unanimous in its decision on that case. Breeden's first cousin, Hugh McColl, CEO and chairman of the board at Bank of America, reports the family believes she was the first woman to argue a case before that Supreme Court.

Early in her childhood, Breeden, known as Patty, proclaimed her exceptional verve for life and declared that she wanted to do everything, see everything, and be everything. By the time she was sixteen years old, she had graduated from high school and was a student at the Women's College of the University of North Carolina. Later, she transferred to the University of South Carolina, where she graduated cum laude and became a law student because she said it had the best graduate program at that institution. In her senior year, she was editor of the *Law Review.*

After Breeden's admission to the bar, she shared office space in Columbia at 1233 Washington Street with Henry W. Edens, who also served as United States assistant district attorney. Edens and Breeden were the appellants in *Schwartz v. Mount Vernon-Woodberry Mills, Inc.,* supra. This was a Workman's Compensation case wherein the appellants argued that, since the disability found was permanent and to the extent of fifty percent of former vision, the award should have been fifty percent of the loss of an eye of normal vision, and, they alleged, the eye had been normal. The court found that the record did not justify this assumption of fact, but complimented "claimant's zealous counsel (one, a fair Portia)."

The year after the Supreme Court rendered a decision in Breeden's appeal, she married a naval officer. The major portion of her career was as an English teacher in Virginia. In 1977, John

Casteen, president of the University of Virginia, called Breeden "the best teacher I've ever seen." At the time of her death on April 20, 1997, she was executive director of the Commonwealth in Education, an international conference on learners and learning.

(44) Sarah Lewis Graydon
admitted October 19, 1944
1921–

Sarah Graydon was on track to become a teacher and writer in her senior year at Hollins College when she decided to become a lawyer. Her father, Clint Graydon, a leading South Carolina attorney who had a large criminal defense practice and was president of the state bar, had a big influence on her. "[B]ut my goal was to study legal actions and learn the political system, not to practice law," Sarah recalls. Toward that end, she entered the University of South Carolina Law School, graduating in 1944, one of only four students in her class. As it turned out, she did not practice law for many years. She married a professor, raised five children, and wrote four books, including a biography of her father. When the youngest of her children was in college, she joined her brother's Columbia law firm.

Now retired, Graydon describes her twenty years of responsibilities in her brother's office as a "general gofer, office manager, and probate specialist." Currently, she is a leader in her Episcopal church and teaches and advises on issues relating to women and African-Americans.

(45) Mary Vann Racey
admitted December 13, 1944
1911–

Mary Vann Racey was a resident of the city of Charleston and a member of the Florida Bar at the time of her admission to the bar of this state. Racey was a 1931 graduate of the law school at the University of Miami. Charleston attorneys Thomas P. Stoney and O. T. Wallace filed letters of recommendation on her behalf with the Supreme Court. She was then renting a home at 404 Huger Street in Charleston, but she did not live in the state long enough to be reported in a city directory.

(46) Hazel Cover Collings
admitted June 12, 1945

Hazel Collings was a graduate of Duke University Law School and a resident of Clemson when she was admitted to the bar. Another attorney included in this history, Corinne B. Cannon, admitted in 1972, reports, "Hazel Collings Poe is a friend and client. I do not know that she ever really practiced after graduation from Duke University. However, she served many years as municipal judge for the city of Clemson and has used her legal background in numerous volunteer activities."

(47) Virginia Smith Morgan
admitted June 12, 1945
1921–

Virginia Smith Morgan was a graduate of Spartanburg High School, Limestone College, and Cumberland University Law School when she was admitted to the bar of this state. Spartanburg attorneys A. E. Tinsley, Thomas Lyles, and Sam Lanham filed letters of recommendation on her behalf with the Supreme Court. She was married to Raleigh attorney Robert B. Morgan, who was also her classmate at Cumberland in Tennessee. They then lived at 253 Oakland Avenue, Spartanburg, but did not remain in the city long enough to be listed in a city directory.

(48) Jean Grist
admitted June 14, 1945
1925–1988

Jean Grist was seven months and twelve days shy of being a legal adult (twenty-one years of age) when she stood before the Supreme Court to take the oath to become an attorney. In anticipation of that day, the state senator from her home county of York, Joseph R. Moss, introduced special legislation for her on February 13, 1945.

The act provided: "That Miss Jean Grist, a minor, be, and she hereby is, permitted to apply for admission to the bar upon her graduation at the law school of the University of South Carolina with the degree of bachelor of laws. The Supreme Court is hereby authorized, upon the proper motion being made to admit the said Miss Jean Grist to all of the privileges granted by the statute laws of South Carolina to persons applying for admission to practice as an attorney at law." This legislation moved swiftly through the General Assembly and was ratified by the governor on February 21, eight days after its introduction. On June 8, each of the five members of the law school graduating class, including Grist, submitted a petition to the Supreme Court asking that Grist "be permitted to sign the roll of attorneys." Their petition was granted and she was admitted. After her admission to the bar, Grist married Mr. Dantzler, a Columbia businessman, and never practiced law. Her classmate, Morris D. Mazursky, recalls that the couple owned Dantzler Appliance on Devine Street in Columbia.

(49) Louise B. Wideman
admitted December 10, 1945
1905–1994

Louise Wideman's professional career began in 1933 as a court reporter in Spartanburg. Following that, she took a position as secretary to Governor I. C. Blackwood (1931–1935). Later, Wideman was promoted to clerk of the House of Representatives Judiciary Committee. This clerkship was a major portion of her professional career, covering a twenty-one-year period from 1935 to 1956. At that time, the Judiciary Committee was composed exclusively of attorneys, some of whom encouraged her to study law. Wideman read law under the tutelage of Professor Charles B. Elliott, a lawyer who taught at the law school and maintained a private practice in Columbia. After Wideman was admitted to the bar, she, too, tutored students who wanted to qualify for the bar examination by studying privately. In the course of her career, she was admitted to practice before the Internal Revenue Tax Court, and for a period of twenty years, Wideman was a pro bono attorney with the Military Draft Board Number 40 in Columbia. The apogee of Wideman's career came in 1956 when Governor George Bell Timmerman (1955–1959) appointed her to the Workman's Compensation Commission. She served in this judicial capacity until her retirement on December 31, 1971.

★ ★ ★

The G.I. Bill of Rights, enacted in 1944, and peace in 1945 brought a wave of returning male and some female veterans to colleges and universities in 1946. By 1947, there were 328 students enrolled in law school at the University of South Carolina in a building adequate for 75. The following year, there were 398 law students. The bar association prevailed upon the university to construct a new law building, and the law faculty began offering three full semesters each year. Most of the veteran students enrolled in this two-year program, which continued until 1956.

The feminist movement, however, became dormant during the Great Depression and World War II. According to the *American Journal of Sociology* 125-130 (September, 1947), the model-type family was then the "semi-patriarchal form in which a dominant husband brings in the bacon." Betty Friedan remembered in *It Changed My Life* (Friedan 1977), "In 1949, nobody had to tell a woman that she wanted a man, but the message began bombarding us from all sides; domestic bliss had suddenly become chic, sophisticated."

The largest number of marriages in any one year in the history of keeping such records in the United States occurred in 1946. Of the twelve women admitted to the bar in the second half of the decade, one-half married attorneys. This was the first occasion of law students marrying law students.

Returning veterans brought with them motivation for change and high hopes for social mobility. One of these veterans, John Wrighten, an African-American, applied for admission to the university's law school on June 30, 1946. His application was not approved, and the following year, a legal action was filed on his behalf. The decision of the court stated that if the state was going to offer a legal education, it must provide a school for Wrighten. His case was not appealed to the United States Supreme Court; however, the state established a law school for African-Americans at the South Carolina College in Orangeburg. No women registered at this law school until the 1960s; but, attorney Cassandra Maxwell, admitted in 1941, became a professor at Orangeburg and, as noted, was consequently the first woman on a law school faculty in this state.

Another memorable event for the legal profession occurred in 1947 when South Carolina tried its last lynching case. The case was heard in Greenville in the Court of General Sessions. A satire of the trial written by the British writer, Rebecca West, appeared in *The New Yorker* on June 14, 1947, titled "Opera in Greenville." Two weeks before its publication, newly admitted attorney, Mary Francis Fazio, included later in this study, joined the firm of one of the defense attorneys, John Bolt Culbertson. West's description of the Greenville courthouse and courtroom could have described any one of the forty-six county courthouses then in South Carolina.

> *This is a singularly hideous building (courthouse) faced with yellow washroom tiles, standing on Main Street, next to the principal hotel. . . . The courtroom is about the size of the famous court at Old Bailey in London. In the body of the courtroom, there are chairs for about three hundred white persons. The front rows were occupied by the thirty-one defendants who were being tried for lynching a Negro early on the morning of February 27 of this year. . . . Nearly all these defendants were exercising a right their state permits to all persons accused of a capital offense. They brought their families with them in court. . . .*
>
> *Behind the defendants and their families sat something under two hundred of such citizens of Greenville as could find the time to attend the trial, which was held during work hours. Some were drawn from the men of the town who are too old or sick to work, or who do not enjoy work and use the courthouse as a club, sitting on the steps, chewing and smoking and looking down on Main Street through the hot, dancing air, when the weather is right for that, and going inside when*

it is better there. . . . Upstairs in the deep gallery sat about a hundred and fifty Negroes, under the care of two white bailiffs. Many of them, too, were court spectators of habit. . . .

The judge, J. Robert Martin, Jr., is very local. He knows all about the rhetoric and opera. His speech arouses wonder as to how the best sort of stenographer, who takes down by sounds and not by sense, is not wholly baffled in the South, where 'You gentlemen must appor-tion your time' is converted into 'Yo g'men must appo'tion yo' taiaime,' with a magnificent vibrato on the diphthongs and strong melodic line to the whole. He is so good that though he is local, he expands the local meaning, and recalls that great Southerners are great men in the whole world. He has humor, but hates a clown.

When the jury returned a verdict of 'not guilty' as to all defen-dants, Judge Martin stood, thought a minute, turned, and walked out of the courtroom. He did not thank the jury, as was his custom.

A South Carolina anachronism, still remaining in 1948, was the distinction of being the only state still disallowing divorce. The big-ticket item on the November 1948 ballot was the presidential race between Harry Truman, Thomas Dewey, and favorite son Dixiecrat, Strom Thurmond. An amendment to permit divorce as a cause of action appeared on the same ballot. Not surprisingly, there was a heavy voter turnout, bringing South Carolina into the twentieth century with 56,014 votes favoring divorce to 41,757 against. The causes of divorce action were based on separation for more than one year, adultery, habitual drunkenness, and physical cruelty. All but eleven counties voted to legalize divorce, and ten of those did not have a resident practicing woman attorney. They were Anderson, Bamberg, Barnwell, Cherokee, Lancaster, Laurens, Oconee, Pickens, Saluda, and Williamsburg. Colleton also voted against divorce. Its only resident woman attorney, Alice Beckett, admitted in 1946, was opposed to the amendment. The divorce amendment was then rati-fied by the General Assembly, and the press reported that the first divorce in this state occurred on June 29, 1949.

The procedure for divorce actions required one party to file for relief in the Court of Common Pleas. This was heard before the master in equity or the circuit judge. Circuit judges routinely heard domestic matters on Saturday mornings. Generally, the practice of the bar was for the plaintiff's attorney to prepare the testimony in advance, and the client would swear to it before the judge. On a rare occasion, a visiting judge would be heard to say, "Don't bring any canned testimony before me." Most of the cases were settled by default.

Lastly, before the end of this decade, the South Carolina Legislature modernized requirements for admission to the bar. Each year, law students had been flocking to the Legislature to persuade their House and Senate members to vote against declaring the diploma privilege null and void. "The students had more influence than the bar association," noted Chief Justice (ret.) Bruce Littlejohn, who was Speaker of the House at that time. "Finally," Littlejohn wrote in *Half Century at the Bench and Bar,* (Littlejohn 1987) "Some wise legislator came up with the idea that the bill should be enacted effective three years hence. This called off the lobbying, and the bill requiring all applicants to stand the bar examination went through without serious contest." This act was approved in April 1948, and applied to those persons who were admitted on December 13, 1950, and after. Lawyers who were then students at the university have told this writer that they believed the motivating force behind the legislation was to question the legal education being offered at the law school in Orangeburg. The two women admitted to the bar in 1946 were not affected by this brouhaha. They had prepared for the bar examination during the war years by reading law.

(50) Alice T. Beckett
admitted June 10, 1946
1908–2000

Born in 1908 in Walterboro, Alice Beckett was one of nine siblings, only five of whom reached maturity. Her father was George Wilkes Beckett, an attorney who qualified to take the Georgia Bar examination by reading law in that state. He established his practice and law office in Beaufort. Alice's work career began after she finished seventh grade; however, she continued her education through high school graduation at the completion of tenth grade. She acquired some business skills at Holy Cross Academy in Washington, D.C., and later at St. Joseph's Academy in Sumter.

Beckett's work experience, for the most part, was in legal offices. She worked part time in her father's office in the late twenties, followed by full-time employment in the Beaufort law office of J. Heyward Jenkins. From there, she returned to Walterboro, where she was a secretary in the law offices of James G. Padgett and James M. Moore for four years.

According to hearsay, while Beckett was at the Padgett and Moore firm, two other lawyers confronted her with allegations that they believed she was practicing law without a license and suggested she take the bar examination. True or not, she made a career change to a civil service position.

During the war years, Beckett was a secretary in the law office of Legge and Gibbs on Broad Street in Charleston, having given up her civil service position to prepare for the bar examination by reading law. She was with this firm for six years, working primarily for Lionel Legge, who later became a justice on the state Supreme Court.

After her admission to the bar, Beckett returned to Walterboro as secretary and legal assistant to Attorney J. C. Lemacks, earning thirty-five dollars a week at his office at 122 Hampton Street, around the corner from the courthouse. Since she was the first woman to practice law in Colleton County, she believed her presence at the bar meetings would put a damper on members' social activities. She had heard that they drank cocktails and played poker. "So, I didn't go," Beckett said. "When I got home, the lady I was staying with said, 'They have a warrant out for you. The sheriff was looking for you. . . . They (the lawyers) say you're one of them now.' I learned to take a drink, but I was very particular about who fixed the drink." The Colleton County Bar Association then had the custom of naming the newest attorney as its secretary and treasurer.

Beckett assumed this responsibility and kept it for twenty-five years, thus relieving new lawyers of the task.

Beckett and Lemacks entered into an agreement that upon his death, she could buy his practice, paying for it over a period of eight years. He died in 1952. Their agreement included the building, files, equipment, furniture, and library. In her practice, she did not try cases, explaining, "Well, I just wasn't that type to get up and talk and fight over something like that. It just wasn't my phase . . . five dollars for a deed, seven dollars and a half for a mortgage, ten dollars for a will. When it went up to twenty-five dollars for a will, we thought we had a gold mine."

Three times Beckett was elected to serve on the Walterboro City Council. She also provided pro bono service to the Catholic Church of Colleton and Beaufort Counties. Beckett retired from active practice at age eighty.

(51) Doris Camille Hutson
admitted June 10, 1946
1925–

Doris Camille Hutson, who always tended to be ahead of schedule, skipped her last year at Orangeburg High School to enter the University of South Carolina, where she traded her last year of college for her first year in law school, graduating in 1944. After reading law in her father's office, she was admitted to the bar by the Supreme Court before she was twenty-one years old. It was only with special permission of the Supreme Court that she was allowed to practice law before her next birthday. Her father, L. A. Hutson, Esquire, had an office located at 121 Middleton Street N.E. in Orangeburg. Upon admission to the bar, she joined him in his practice.

Hutson heard about an open position with the American Mission in Greece Corps of Engineers while she was visiting in Washington, D.C. She qualified for this position and was accepted. In March 1948, she wrote from Greece, "I'm meeting all the ministers and (they) are still shocked over the fact that they have women lawyers in America." She spent the greater portion of her professional time while in Greece in the labor relations section, adjusting labor difficulties and differences among and between employees, both American and Greek. When the mission was closed in 1949, she took a three-month tour of the continent before she entered law school at the University of Michigan, where she graduated with a doctor of jurisprudence in 1952.

During graduate school, Hutson met and married Ralph G. Dunn, M.D. Since her graduation, they have lived in Houston, Texas. She was admitted to the practice of law in Texas in 1963, where she became board certified in family law. In 1984, Camile Hutson was the first woman and first Republican elected to be an associate justice of the state of Texas in the First Court of Appeals. About sixty percent of the cases this court considers are criminal and the rest are civil. She is quoted as saying she "decided to seek the office after the higher court decision on a case, which involved a detailed property division, cost her client more than ten thousand dollars in interest." The election was by popular vote, but she refused to be endorsed by any special-interest groups. During the political campaign for the judgeship, Dunn stated she believed that many judges hearing cases on property and family law do not have a strong working knowledge of the law in those areas.

"When a case is brought to me, sometimes they roll it in on a cart. My husband is an ophthalmologist, and I've changed glasses three times in six years," she said when seeking re-election. Judge Dunn is a member of numerous professional organizations, and she and her husband are the parents of three children. She continues to keep in touch with her relations and many friends who live in Orangeburg.

(52) Julia Anne Kleckly
admitted January 28, 1947

Actually, Julia Anne Kleckly graduated from law school in December 1946, but lawyers in that class were not admitted to the bar until January 28, 1947. Kleckly grew up in the Shandon area of Columbia and took her undergraduate degree at the university. While a freshman in law school, this exceptionally beautiful woman was elected Miss Garnet and Black. A full-page color photograph of her appeared in the yearbook.

When Kleckly graduated from law school, the dean asked her to fill in as law school librarian until Sarah Glymph Wilcox, admitted in 1936, could assume that responsibility. Kleckly had already accepted a position as legal assistant in the Anti-Trust Division of the United States Justice Department; however, the federal post would not begin until October 1947. Her expectation upon being admitted to the bar was that she would have a legal career in Washington, winning battles for "the people." However, those plans went awry.

One of the responsibilities of the librarian was to teach the first-semester law students a course in legal history and bibliography. Sidney S. Tison, a recently returned war veteran, was in Kleckly's class of one hundred freshmen. The two were attracted to each other and began dating.

After Wilcox became the librarian, Kleckly joined the office of chief attorney for the Anti-Trust Division in Cleveland, Ohio. She had an assignment to assist in a futile legal action against the plumbing industry. The government lawyers consumed six months to present the case to the federal judge, who then dismissed it. Meanwhile, the romance with Tison progressed and Kleckly gladly returned to Columbia. They were married in November 1947. While he finished his last year in law school, she worked in the right-of-way division of the South Carolina Highway Department.

The two lawyers, bride and groom, moved to Bennettsville and joined his father's law firm, where she checked titles (to real estate), drafted pleadings, and worked on a brief for the Supreme Court.

We opened another Tison and Tison law office in Hartsville. I was never a partner. I was an associate because Sidney didn't want me to be responsible for any liability to which the firm might be subjected. He did say that my having a law degree was more valuable to the firm than having an insurance policy. I was always involved in the firm. I handled all the title work—checking titles, writing certificates of title. Sidney and I often discussed options and ways to handle many cases

with me acting as his sounding board. He was the consummate nego-
tiator and a visionary. I was the one who handled the day-to-day
details, bookkeeping, accounts, et cetera, as well as filling in as secretary and receptionist when needed or necessary.

When Sidney's health became a constant concern in late 1991, I
was lawyer, secretary, and care giver. He continued to go to the office
until about three weeks before his death on February 23, 1999. I kept
the office open throughout that year.

I had the best of all worlds—I was able to combine marriage,
motherhood (four children), as well as to keep my legal aspirations
current.

(53) Elizabeth Blair Haynsworth
admitted January 28, 1947
1920–1996

Elizabeth Blair Haynsworth was a member of a Greenville family long prominent in Carolina legal circles. Her grandfather, Harry J.
Haynsworth, established his law firm in 1887 and was president of
the state bar in 1904. Her brother, Clement Furman Haynsworth,
was a justice of the United States Fourth Circuit Court of Appeals.

Would-be Portia, Haynsworth completed her undergraduate
education at Furman University before applying to Harvard Law
School, her grandfather's alma mater. She was rejected because, at
that time, Harvard Law School did not accept women. She was then
accepted to the law school at the University of Virginia. Her daughter, Elsie Haynsworth Taylor Owens, tells: "One of mother's law
school professors wrote a friend who taught at Harvard that in his
constitutional law class, he had the finest legal mind that he had ever
taught, 'but, unfortunately, it was in the head of a woman.' This
Harvard professor sent the letter to her grandfather." After graduation, she took a position with a New York Wall Street law firm. Upon
her admission to the bar of this state, she became associated with the
Haynsworth firm in Greenville. A year later, she married Benjamin
Walter Taylor of Columbia, where the couple made their home.
During her first year in Columbia, Elizabeth Haynsworth Taylor was

manager of Lawyers Title Insurance Company. After she left that position, she did not continue to practice law. She devoted her life to raising her children.

(54) Ruth I. Young
admitted June 2, 1947

Ruth I. Young identified Philadelphia, Pennsylvania, as her home when she was admitted to the practice of law in South Carolina.

"Ruth I. Young was in law school when I was," says Julia Kleckly Tison. "She had been in service, the army I think. This background led to quite a different experience from the one I had when Dean Frierson and Judge Whaley apologized to me for having to discuss 'unladylike subjects' presented in the criminal case books. However, I have been told that one of my favorite professors, Coleman Karesh, treated her 'like one of the boys' and felt she enjoyed the 'off-color' jokes as much as the men.

"She married one of Sidney's law school classmates whose name was Orville L. Rodgers. He had been a football player at The Citadel, and he looked the part."

Another lawyer, Mary Francis Fazio Hayes, says, "Ruth Young was my roommate during first-year law. She married Orville Rodgers sometime after graduation and, I believe, moved to Florida. I have lost contact with her."

(55) Mary Francis Fazio
admitted June 2, 1947

Mary Francis Fazio took her undergraduate studies at Furman and then was in the first class of the South Carolina Law School that included veterans. She was admitted to the bar on June 2, and two weeks later, she was one of four lawyers in the Greenville firm of John Bolt Culbertson, who "had a busy practice. . . . We used 'Mr.' in our office for all clients," she said.

The New Yorker article (cited previously) describing the last lynching trial included a description of John Bolt Culbertson. "He has a great reputation in the South as a liberal. He is the local attorney for the Congress of Industrial Organization labor union and he worked actively for it. . . . He is one of the very few who shakes hands with Negroes and gives them the prefix of Mr. or Mrs. or Miss."

In a letter to me, Mary Fazio Hayes wrote, "My (favorite) classmate, J. Trus Hayes, Jr. and I were married December 14, 1947. We have been in the same office at 103 North Railroad Avenue in Dillon since. We practiced law together as Hayes and Hayes until his death on July 18, 1995. I still come to the office every day and truly enjoy my work, which is mainly real estate, probate, and some corporate work. I no longer go to family court. There is no distinction as to 'women lawyers' or 'men lawyers.' We were like Gertrude Stein's rose! The 1946 code stated 'any able bodied man who fails to support his wife and children . . .'"

Later by phone, Hayes informed me, "Our daughter, Mary Jean Hayes, is a district attorney in Winston-Salem, North Carolina."

(56) Caroline Ray
admitted June 12, 1947
1910–

Caroline Ray moved to Columbia in September 1946 and was admitted to the bar of this state upon the recommendation of several local lawyers—Samuel R. Preston, Milledge T. Ott, Charles F. Cooper, and Louise Wideman. Her original home was in Chilton County, Alabama. Ray graduated from the law school of the National University in Washington, D.C., and held a position with the U.S. government in the nation's capital before relocating to South Carolina. While in Columbia, she lived at 512 Tyler Street, but did not remain in the city long enough to be noted in its city directory.

(57) Mary Bruton
admitted October 27, 1947
1909–1993

Mary Bruton was admitted to the bar of this state in the same ceremony as her husband, John C. Bruton. The newspaper announcing the opening of their office in Columbia noted that he was reared there and she was from Winnsboro. Before their move to Columbia, both had been attorneys in the New York Wall Street firm of Sullivan and Cromwell, where she specialized in corporate law. She was admitted to the New York Bar in 1940. Sullivan and Cromwell presented John Bruton with a gold watch on the occasion of his leaving that firm, but his wife did not receive one.

Mary Winn Bruton graduated from Barnard College and New York University Law School, where she was a member of its scholastic society. She took graduate work in international law at Columbia University. Later, she was a member of the staff of the New York office of the Carnegie Endowment for International Peace and also took special staff assignments in London, England, and Geneva, Switzerland.

This couple opened their Columbia law office in the Carolina Life Building at 1203 Gervais Street. Five years later, he became a law partner in the firm of Boyd, Bruton, and Lumkin, which was then located in the Barringer Building at 1330 Main Street. She is identified as an associate in that firm. Beginning in 1971, the city directories ceased listing their names as members of this state's bar.

(58) Eleanor Toole Going
admitted June 2, 1948

Eleanor Toole Going is the daughter of Frampton W. Toole, admitted to the bar in 1913, who practiced law in Aiken with his father, Gasper L. Toole, admitted to the bar in 1899. Her two brothers, Frampton, Jr., and Gasper, III, as well as her nephew, Frampton, III, are still with this firm.

When Eleanor Toole graduated from Converse College in 1943, she joined the Women Accepted for Volunteer Emergency Service (the WAVES) and was sent to Smith College for her midshipman training. Upon completion of this program, she was assigned to the Sixth Naval District Headquarters, first located in the Fort Sumter Hotel, then at the Charleston Naval Base. After she was discharged from the service, she enrolled in law school at the university. There she met, and on September 15, 1948, married a classmate, Walter F. Going. Upon admission to the bar, they opened their partnership in Columbia at 1338 Main Street. In the firm, Eleanor, who worked full time, was responsible for the real estate transactions, action to clear titles to land, and foreclosure proceedings. Both she and her husband retired in 1986. Their daughter, Mary Going McIntosh, is currently an attorney in the legal department of Wachovia Bank in Columbia.

(59) Mary Stewart
admitted June 9, 1949
1926–1996

"A descendent of a long line of lawyers" is how Harvey Stewart describes his sister, Mary Nancye Stewart. Their father was Roach Sidney Stewart of the Lancaster Bar, and a partner in the firm of Williams and Stewart, where he represented Duke Power Company. He was also a member of the state Senate.

D. Reese Williams of the Richmond Bar, and grandson of Stewart's partner, knew Mary and recalls:

> *I have pleasant memories of Mary and the years from the mid-forties through the fifties when I knew her best. I was ten years Mary's junior, an impressionable difference, at a time when lawyers interested me almost as much as they do now and what interested me most about Mary was that she was nice to me and pretty.*
>
> *I remember that Mary often was in the Lancaster office of Williams and Stewart, the firm of my grandfather and Colonel Roach Stewart, her father. When I was young, I often spent time there after school and at the courthouse. Mary worked there—perhaps as a clerk—before she went to law school. I do not recall the date of Colonel Stewart's death and cannot say whether Mary worked as a lawyer for Williams and Stewart or for its successor . . . only that she did work as a lawyer. The office was a large room over a store on Main Street, like the reading room of a library, walls of books in sectional book cases with glass doors and several standing-height reading tables, with lawyers and stenographers (not secretaries) scattered around the*

room at desks and no privacy. Mary did research and writing, title and probate—as everyone did—and was in court either with my father or Colonel Stewart on several occasions that I remember. I often watched trials at the courthouse where Colonel Stewart was outstanding. He took Mary and me with him to the legislature and on other business trips occasionally. After Colonel Stewart died, my father and Ed Parler formed a partnership and I am sure Mary found small-town Lancaster confining. She moved to Atlanta while I was in prep school there.

I have asked some of her surviving contemporaries to tell me what they remember about Mary and they simply confirm that no one thought there was anything unusual about Mary becoming a lawyer and thus there was little interest in the specific work she did.

Before Stewart enrolled at the University of South Carolina Law School, she had graduated from Duke University with a degree in English. Following law school, she practiced two years in Lancaster. Her brother further recalls, "Mary would go to the courthouse and gather information needed for prosecution or defense, write it up, and another lawyer would present it. Mary was intelligent and was a member of Mensa." She left Lancaster to go to Atlanta, accepting a position with the Internal Revenue Service, where her brother believes she remained for ten years. She then relocated to Hollywood, Florida, and was admitted to that state's bar.

In this milieu, the brilliant and perhaps somewhat unconventional Mary Stewart thrived. She had a successful practice primarily in real estate matters and a long-term relationship with a man whom she never married. Not until late in life did she return to Lancaster, where she died in 1996.

(60) Jacqueline McKenzie Rainwater
admitted June 9, 1949

Jacqueline Rainwater lives in Bennettsville and does not practice law. Judge Edward B. Cottingham knows her personally and reports that she graduated from the University of Virginia Law School before she took the bar examination in South Carolina and has been a distinguished school teacher in Bennettsville.

The *Lawyer's Desk Book* lists her home address; however, she has not responded to letters of professional inquiry.

The twenty-nine women admitted to the bar in the forties comprise the largest number in any decade covered by this study—less than half that many became attorneys in the decade of the 1950s. Conventionalism, not distinctiveness, was the path chosen for the most part even by educated women of the fifties.

Judith Greenberg, 1940.

Barbara Burt Brown, 1940.

Opal Kelly Hesse, 1941.

Myrtle Holcombe, 1941.

Thomasine Grayson Mason, 1941.

Cassandra E. Maxwell, 1941.

Sarah E. Leverette, 1943.

Edith Pratt Breeden, 1944.

Sarah L. Graydon, 1944.

Jean Grist, 1945.

Louise B. Wideman, 1945.

Alice T. Beckett, 1946.

Doris Camille Hutson, 1946.

Julia Anne Kleckly, 1947.

Elizabeth B. Haynsworth, 1947.

Mary Bruton, 1947.

Mary Stewart, 1949.

~ Five ~
Good Manners, Pearls, and High Heels

Women's aspirations shifted in two directions simultaneously during the mid-twentieth century. There was a visible return to domesticity and a subtle movement into the work force. The publicized domestic ideal appeared to be the most prevalent. It was an era of limited professional expectations. Good manners, pearls, and high heels were the cachet of the aspiring professional woman. Early marriages and young families prevailed. During this decade, more women married between the ages of fifteen and nineteen than in any comparable period, and consequently, there was a surge in the birthrate, which lasted until 1957.

Hugh Hefner, publisher of *Playboy* magazine, wrote in its twenty-fifth anniversary edition in 1975, "The early fifties was an era of conformity and repression—of Eisenhower and Senator Joe McCarthy—the result of two decades of depression and war. But it was also a period of reawaking in America with a re-emphasis on the importance of the individual, on his rights and opportunities in a free society—a period of increasing affluence and leisure time."

I was among the relatively few women who entered the professional world during this decade. At the time, I felt that I was getting some mixed signals about legitimacy as a female wage earner. Certainly, there were occasions when I felt socially out of place.

Historian Dr. John Hammond Moore, in the book *Southern Homefront* (Moore 1998), described the southern woman's pedestal of the 1860s as a place "where women were praised as saints and saviors one moment and then, in the next, told very firmly to remember their true place in the social pecking order." There was little change ninety years later.

Resistance to change notwithstanding, modernization did take place during the 1950s. From 1895 to the current decade, all persons who had taken a constitutional oath, including all lawyers, had to swear, upon their admission to the bar, not to settle disputes by dueling. At the inauguration of James F. Byrnes as governor of South Carolina in 1951, he took the customary and antiquated oath not to settle disputes in that fashion. Byrnes had previously held prestigious positions as justice of the Supreme Court of the United States and as secretary of state among others. Consequently, many of his Washington colleagues attended his inauguration. Chief Justice (ret.) Bruce Littlejohn commented in his book *Political Memories* that, "It is said that the dueling oath was removed from the Constitution upon the insistence of James F. Byrnes. . . . The story goes that some of Byrnes' friends from Washington came to the inauguration and teased him about having to swear that he would not participate in a duel. He seemed embarrassed about it and as a result, advocated and helped to bring about the elimination of this provision from the Constitution." In 1954, an amendment to the 1895 constitution of this state, Section 26, Article III, was on the November general election ballot, proposing to eliminate from the oath that portion regarding dueling. The electorate gave it a favorable vote, and the General Assembly ratified the change in February 1955 by Act Number 24. Then, Section 26, Article III, was changed to read: "The Oath of Office to be Taken . . . 'I do solemnly swear (or affirm) that I am duly qualified, according to the Constitution of this State, to exercise the duties of the office to which I have been elected or appointed, and that I will, to the best of my ability, discharge the duties thereof, and preserve, protect, and defend the Constitution of this state and of the United States. So help me God.' "

Another event in 1954, of considerably greater significance, was the United States Supreme Court's decision ruling the doctrine of "separate but equal" unconstitutional. Of course, this decision had historic and dramatic impacts on public education nationwide. It is noteworthy that this marked the beginning of the end for the law school for African-Americans at South Carolina State College. Henceforth, the University of South Carolina was required to admit black applicants.

Pushing South Carolina's jury system to modernization was the Congressional Public Law 85-315, enacted September 9, 1957, and titled: "To provide means of further securing and protecting the civil rights of persons within the jurisdiction of the United States." It is popularly known as the Civil Rights Act of 1957. Section 152 of that law amended Section 1861 of the then-existing code to state: "Qualifications of Federal jurors. Any citizen of the United States who has attained the age of twenty-one and who has resided for a period of one year within the judicial district is competent to serve as a grand or petit juror unless . . . he has been convicted of a crime punishable by imprisonment of more than one year . . . he is unable to read . . . he is incapable by reason of mental or physical infirmities to render efficient jury service."

Assistant Federal District Attorney Arthur G. Howe was prepared to present criminal indictments before Judge George Bell Timmerman when he received a copy of Public Law 85-315. Howe concluded that this legislation required the names of women as well as African-Americans to be in the federal jury venire. He then prepared just such an order for Judge Timmerman, who was holding court in Columbia, and Judge Timmerman signed it reluctantly, Howe recalls. Timmerman quashed the pending indictments.

At that time, the federal clerk of court was required to "canvas" the district for the names of prospective jurors. Howe says the clerk, Ernest F. Allen, solicited the names from lawyers and preachers. Howe saw Allen specifically including the names of African-Americans in the lists of petit and grand jury, and told Clerk Allen,

"You can not intentionally include African-Americans for jury duty just as you can not intentionally exclude them." After reflection, in conversation with me in October 2000, Howe said he believed Clerk Allen probably intentionally included women's names in the jury pool and, in fact, women did then begin to serve on federal juries. Not until the next decade, however, were women on state or local juries.

Eliminating the custom of "reading law" was another modernization that took place. On June 18, 1957, Governor Byrnes signed legislation giving the Supreme Court the inherent power to fix qualifications for admission to the bar (50 Statutes at Large 553). November 30 of that year, the court established the rule that no person shall be admitted to the practice of law who was not a graduate of the law school of the University of South Carolina, the law school of South Carolina State College, or a law school approved by the council of legal education of the American Bar Association. These rules further provided a window of time to accept those individuals already engaged in reading law. This provision states:

Provided, further, any person who prior to January 1, 1957, commenced the study of law in a law office under the direction of a member of the bar of this State, as heretofore authorized by Rule 30 of this Court, may on or before April 1, 1958, apply to the Supreme Court for a variation of relaxation of requirement four of the above rule as to graduation from a law school. The granting or refusal of such application shall rest in the discretion of the Supreme Court.

The revised wording of the oath required of new lawyers eliminated anachronisms.

I do solemnly swear (or affirm) I am duly qualified, according to the Constitution of this State, to exercise the duties of the office to which I have been appointed, and that I will, to the best of my ability, discharge the duties thereof, and preserve, protect, and defend the Constitution of this State and the United States.

I will maintain the respect due to courts of justice and judicial officers.

I will not counsel or maintain any suit or proceeding which shall appear to me to be unjust, nor any defense except such I believe to be honestly debatable under the law of the land, but this obligation shall not prevent me from defending a person charged with crime in any case.

I will employ for the purpose of maintaining the causes confided to me such means only as are consistent with truth and honor, and will never seek to mislead the judge or jury by any artifice or false statement of fact or law.

I will respect the confidence and preserve inviolate the secrets of my client, and will accept no compensation in connection with his business except from him or with his knowledge and approval.

I will abstain from all offensive personalities, and advance no fact prejudicial to the honor or reputation of a party or witness, unless required by the justice of the cause with which I am charged.

I will never reject, from any consideration personal to myself the cause of the defenseless or oppressed, or delay any man's cause for lucre or malice.

I will abstain from direct or indirect solicitation of employment, to institute, prosecute, or defend against any claim, action, or cause of action.

So help me God.

Procedures described as innovations in the 1950s were taken for granted by today's younger lawyers. Medieval relics and vestiges of traditions from London's Inns of Court remained in local courts and in the legal profession during the 1950s. During this decade, I entered the legal profession, paying close attention to the unwritten rituals and taking pleasure in the symbols reminiscent of early English trials because I thought heaven was in London's Inns of Court. Additionally, I learned how a rural county adapted life at the courthouse to its small-town ways.

A legacy from London's criminal court of Old Bailey was the dock—a wooden enclosure about four or five feet square with the upper half of the box open. There, an alleged criminal would sit or stand during his arraignment, while the charge was read to him and he was asked if he pleads "guilty" or "not guilty." Circuit Court Rule Number 35 prescribed the use of the dock. The Supreme Court abolished this rule in January 1984. At one time, all forty-six county courthouses had a dock. Most of them were eliminated in new construction or removed in remodeling of courthouses in the last half of the twentieth century. Richland County had a portable one, a dock on wheels that could be rolled in and out of the courtroom. Hurricane Hugo, that well-known criminal, destroyed Charleston's dock by dropping a ceiling and roof on it. Spartanburg eliminated its dock when it built a new courthouse in 1958.

Another fixture in the old courtrooms eliminated by modernization of courthouses was the brass spittoon. One was next to the table of the attorneys for the plaintiff and another for the defendant. Spittoons were also near the spectators. Lawyers would not smoke during a trial, but they could chew and spit in the receptacle. As soon as the judge walked out of the courtroom, attorneys lit up their cigarettes and brass cuspidors became ashtrays. If the judge wanted to smoke during the trial, he stood in the doorway of the courtroom and blew his smoke into the hall.

A bailiff in the Cherokee County courthouse in the 1950s still carried a seven-foot wooden staff to quiet disturbances in the courtroom. If spectators whispered too loudly or laughed, he would demand order by hitting the staff resoundingly against the floor several times. Oconee County had the last court crier in the state, a man named Billy Hunt, who was an officer of the court, announcing the beginning of trials, stating the matters about to be transacted, names of the jurors, witnesses, and parties. Hunt would declare when a witness was sworn, proclaim silence as well as declare adjournments and recesses. "He loved to step to the courtroom door and three times call out the name of the absent defendant, then turn and announce to the court that his call had not been answered," says Chief Justice (ret.) Bruce Littlejohn. Charleston lawyer Larry Duffy also remembers that the Hampton County courthouse had a crier.

The South Carolina Code at 14-7-270 provides that a child under the age of ten or a totally blind person is qualified to draw the jury, whose names of individuals are encased in a capsule and placed in a drum. Most of the courts used a boy under the age of ten to draw their juries, although a few used a blind man. Most of the time, Charleston juries were drawn by the latter, but from time to time, a child would be used. On one occasion, I nodded to the blind jury-man as I took a step to join him in the courthouse elevator and strangely, he nodded back. The only South Carolina jury girl child that I have been able to identify is Pamela Hughes, now a school principal in Berkeley County.

The clerk of court and lawyers used to have a callous habit of addressing the jury-drawing blind man as simply, "The blind man." A clerk would announce to the courtroom, "Somebody go get the blind man. He's outside smoking and it's time to draw the jury," or "The blind man will now draw the jury." When A. Arthur Rosenblum was solicitor in Berkeley and Charleston Counties in the early 1980s, he was the first to instruct the clerk that he must address the blind man by his name.

The custom now used in most courts is for the clerk to announce, "There being no objection," (that is, no one objecting to the fact that a child or blind person is not present) "the clerk will draw the jury."

All state court terms opened with prayer. Usually, a local minister would be present on the request of the judge or the clerk. Once, when Judge Frank Epps was holding a term of criminal court in Aiken, neither the judge nor the clerk had invited a minister. In open court, Judge Epps asked, "Is there a preacher present in the courtroom who would be willing to step forward and begin this court term with a prayer?" One tall preacher arose and holding his hat reverently over his heart, bowed low toward the bench and offered his services. The judge said, "All rise, be up standing." The preacher's dignified, melodic voice asked God to render mercy in that courtroom. (He did not pray for justice.) It was only later that Judge Epps became embarrassed to learn that this preacher was one of the defendants who was summoned to appear before the bench that day. The preacher's case was transferred to another term of court.

Most of the time, those present in the courtroom would rise and stand for the invocation, but sometimes all the citizens would continue sitting, bow their heads, and close their eyes. There were no kneelers.

Prayer in the state's federal court was raised as a constitutional issue in a case that arose in the court of Judge Solomon Blatt, Jr. (*The United States v. Walker,* 696 Fed.(2) 277 (1982). Upon appeal to the Fourth Circuit Court, Judge Clement Haynsworth wrote for the court, "The practice, however, is a needless risky one. Because each minister composes his own prayer, its content is beyond control of the judge . . ."

Before the chief administrative judges took control of the civil court docket, it was managed by the local bar associations. The week before a term of court was to begin, the bar associations would meet and either the president or the clerk would read aloud the names of the pending cases and ask if they were ready for trial. Sometimes an attorney would ask for a day certain to accommodate out-of-town witnesses, but most of the time the plaintiff's attorney would answer, "Ready for trial." The defendant's attorney would hem and haw and slowly say, "Well, I need to make a motion for continuance." It was not uncommon for a bar president of a small county to ring up the judge and report that all the cases had been settled or continued.

The court reporter's responsibility was to take each word of a trial down in shorthand on a standard five-inch by eight-inch short-hand notebook held together by a spiral binding at the top. Reporters generally could read back any portion of the record at the request of a judge or an attorney. There was at least one occasion in Walhalla when the court reporter did not take down the words of the judge's charge to instruct the jury. As he rendered his charge, the circuit judge noticed that this court reporter was not taking his words down in shorthand. After the jury had retired to consider the verdict, the judge called the court reporter into his chambers. After a little small talk, the judge explained to the reporter what he had observed. The court reporter replied, "Judge, I can type you up a bet-ter charge than you have ever given." It was a giant step forward when stenotype machines came on the market.

One anachronism of the bar that has survived into the twenty-first century is the practice of attorneys identifying every case by the names of the opposing lawyers, i.e. *Sue E. Erwin, Esquire vs. Eugene F. Rogers, Esquire,* or *Corky Erwin vs. Gene Rogers.*

Each county bar association had its custom for respecting the death and funeral of a fellow attorney. Until sometime in the 1960s, the Charleston County courthouse closed for the funeral of a lawyer as an officer of the court. I remember promising the clerks in the probate court that I would have my funeral on a Friday afternoon. This tradition was eventually changed from closing the whole courthouse to having the courtrooms stand at ease during the hours of a funeral for a lawyer. In addition, two officers of the Charleston Bar Association would personally offer condolences to the bereaved family.

The Berkeley County courthouse had a tradition that I believe was unique and not seen in the other forty-five courthouses in the state. The practice started because there was racial segregation in eating establishments. Criminal court terms were every spring and fall, during which time some enterprising African-Americans would set up a portable eating establishment on the courthouse lawn. They cooked and served rice and fish sandwiches. Out of a cooler, they sold milk, orange juice, and Cokes.

Several cooks would begin about 10 A.M. by frying fish and cooking rice in an old wash pot on their cast-iron wood-burning stove. The old range had a stovepipe, but the smell was always in the courtroom. When Oxford-educated James A. Spruill was presiding in Moncks Corner, he called Solicitor Arthur Howe into his chambers and asked, "What is that smell in the courtroom?"

I witnessed this scene, and local attorneys Norman West and Bill Shipley were also very familiar with this outdoor cafe. Customers took their lunch and sat on the courthouse steps or on the outside benches to eat. The sandwiches seemed to be mostly bread with the fish sticking out of two sides. The clientele had a choice of condiments—mayo or ketchup. When Greenville Judge Frank Epps was holding court, he got in line to eat a fish sandwich. White lawyers began to take their lunch there also. A good many of the criminal arrests in Berkeley County during this period were hunting and fishing violations. The portable eatery went out of business in the late 1960s.

The Berkeley clerks of court, "Buster" Williams and Calvin N. Clark, kept a tin tub in their office full of ice and free Cokes for the lawyers and the judge. Drink machines were an innovation yet to come. The jury room had such thin walls that the lawyer and the judge could listen to their deliberations. "Sometime they would get in a right spirited discussion," said Attorney Bill Shipley. The floor in the 1896 courtroom had been laid with green lumber and as it dried out, it had shrunk. Folks in the courtroom could see through the cracks and watch what was going on in the sheriff's office below the court.

At the beginning of the decade, sixteen women in South Carolina were working full time in the private practice of law. Thirteen more became attorneys during the fifties, but only nine used their legal education in their occupation. The sixteen included Perry, Charles, Sledge, Beaty, Wilburn, Townsend, Huggins, Eldridge, White, Mason, Maxwell, Beckett, Tison, Hayes, Bruton, and Going.

I had the general perception that women lawyers did not do contested litigation, but after studying these biographies, I found this was not correct. However, this unwritten law was confirmed in a 1958 publication by the United States Department of Labor written by Verna Elizabeth Griffin. This United States Printing Office booklet advised women lawyers to concentrate on "real estate, domestic relations work, women and juvenile legal problems, probate work, and patent law."

(61) Milly S. Dufour
admitted June 15, 1951

Milly S. Dufour was born into a family firm of lawyers. Her father, brother, sister, and brother-in-law are attorneys, and her mother was their legal secretary. The family partnership is in Murfreesboro, Tennessee, and now includes two of her nephews. "It was a typical small-town practice—no specialization . . . mainly civil," says Dufour. "As a child, Daddy and Mother rarely discussed the legal business in front of us. However, as we grew older, we asked more questions and sort of gravitated to the office after school. I particularly enjoyed going to the courthouse and talking with the people there. To keep me occupied, Daddy or Mother would frequently have me check some things in the register's office or probate court, but at that time, I still intended to be a psychiatrist and not a lawyer.

"I met Alfred E. Dufour at Duke Law School, and he was from Charleston. We were married in August 1950, and we graduated from Duke in June 1951. We hung out our shingle in Aiken that July and named our firm, Dufour and Dufour."

Alfred had received a good offer to join a firm, but at that time, Milly was offered secretarial positions. "The major reason for this was that no firm had positions for both of us," she said. "The reason we settled on Aiken was because the bomb plant was being built there then, and my husband had a cousin who lived in Graniteville. We talked with Strom Thurmond, and to other lawyers there who were receptive to the idea," Dufour said. Their firm handled all types of cases, including personal injury, domestic relations, property management, estate planning, and appointments to criminal cases. Milly reports that she never had any apprehension that being a woman precluded her trying cases in the courtroom.

"The advantages of a husband and wife being in the same profession outweigh the disadvantages," said Alfred Dufour. "Advantages are being able to understand each other's hours and getting to see each other during the day—not that we were under each other's feet all the time. But if we had a hard day, our moods were more or less equal. We could be tired together.

"The only disadvantage I can think of is that Milly is very conscious of her responsibilities at home. Being a lawyer is a full-time job.

"Sometimes she has obligations at the office that keep her from doing things she feels needed to be done at home. This worries her sometimes," he continued.

Milly went to work early and left early so she could be home when their sons returned from school. Alfred, on the other hand, went to work late and left late because he said he worked better on that schedule. They loved working together and recommended it to any couple that had the opportunity.

In the mid-fifties, Milly Dufour became the first attorney in the state to try a jury case wearing a maternity dress. The maternity style then was to have an opening in the front of the skirt covered by a smock. Milly is just barely five feet tall, and this diminutive attorney wore stiletto heels for that trial! George "Buck" Grant was the opposing lawyer, and he protested with a smile, "It isn't fair!" The jury brought in a favorable verdict for Milly's client.

In addition to membership in the county, state, and American bar associations, Milly has served as state bar examiner, president, and director of the Bar Foundation, as well as other bar association responsibilities.

Alfred E. Dufour is now deceased. One son is now in the firm of Dufour and Dufour, where his mother is "of counsel."

(62) Irene Getter Krugman

admitted June 11, 1952

When licensed to practice law, Irene Krugman, holding a cum laude undergraduate degree as well as a law degree from the University of South Carolina, hung out her shingle over her father's Columbia furniture store. Now she is second in a law partnership with her son in the Aiken firm familiarly known as "Morris, Rudnick, and Mamma."

"I did not have any expectations of the legal career. I wanted to become a lawyer so that I would have an interesting profession and help others. When interviewed by the press as a student, I remember stating that the reason I wanted to become a lawyer was to see that justice was done. It was difficult, if not impossible, to obtain a job when I graduated, so I opened my own office for two years until I married and moved to Aiken," Irene said.

When Irene married Harold Rudnick, an Aiken furniture merchant, she opened her new office in his store at 224 Park Place. On their honeymoon, Harold told her he wanted her to sue a chap who had skipped out of town owing him five hundred dollars. The man left owning real estate in Aiken, so Irene got a judgment levied on his real property and he paid the bill.

Known for her sense of humor, Irene claimed that her law practice specialized "in anything over five dollars." She recalls making necessary numerous copies for a partition action on an old mimeograph machine, which she kept on her kitchen table. Her infant son watched the process and still became a lawyer.

"When I began practicing law, there was no unified court system, and Aiken County had a domestic relations court, but it had no way to enforce child support payments. To collect unpaid child support, a party had to file another legal action in the court," recalls Irene.

The post office once delivered a letter to her with this address: "Lady Lawyer that had the Repossession Case in North Augusta Municipal Court." The letter contained her fee. "When we got to that court, the magistrate complained because he had to quit watching Perry Mason on the television to try the case," Irene remarked wryly.

In addition to her law practice, Irene has been on the faculty of Warrenville Elementary School and the University of South Carolina-Aiken.

In one of her law classes, she was teaching about "unjust enrichment" and recalls using that term five times. On a test, she asked the students to define the term. One answer submitted was "unjust in Richmond." On another test, she asked the students to define the term "easement." An answer given was, "where one is making payments and start off making a lesser amount and gradually increasing the amount of the payment."

Irene Rudnick has also served as Aiken County superintendent of education and as a member of the General Assembly, 1972 to 1978, 1980 to 1984, and 1986 to 1994. While in the Legislature, she served as vice president of the prestigious House Judiciary Committee.

Both her son and daughter are attorneys.

"While I've not made a lot of money in the practice of law, I've had a lot fun," Irene concludes.

(63) Eva Roberta Hightower
admitted November 13, 1952

Eva Hightower's daughter, Barbara E. Brunson, Esquire, is the senior counsel in the legal department of the Fleet Mortgage Company of Columbia. Brunson has written her mother's professional biography.

> *Eva Brunson graduated from the University of South Carolina Law School in 1952, but the story of Mother's career began earlier. My mother was reared in rural Barnwell County; she was one of twelve children of whom seven were girls. Her parents taught her to value education and to believe that she could achieve whatever goal she chose. While enrolled as an undergraduate student at the University of South Carolina, at the advent of World War II, my mother decided to enlist in the Navy. She excelled in her basic training and was assigned to work at the Pentagon. As a chief yeoman in the WAVES, she worked in the military government section of the office of the Chief of Naval Operations. There she participated in planning procedures for the governing of islands in the Pacific where the Navy had jurisdiction.*
>
> *Her experiences at the Pentagon fostered her desire to continue her education. After the war, she returned to South Carolina to finish her undergraduate degree and law school. An interesting story from this time in her life concerns her application to the Veterans' Administration for proceeds from the G.I. Bill to pay for attending law school. The first administrator with whom she spoke refused to approve an application by a woman for funds to attend law school. However, my mother persisted and the man's supervisor approved her application.*

A law school classmate of Eva, Bob Carpenter, recalls their class in contracts with Professor James Sumner. Carpenter says, "Slim Jim Sumner was hard as nails. He had been a tank commander under General George C. Patton in World War II and had mastered the strategy of the lightning attack, which he used on students. He did not think women should be in law school and he gave Eva a tough time, but Eva gave as good as she got."

Her daughter wrote:

After admittance to the bar, she began her practice in Williston with Frampton Harper, a general practitioner, and was there until she married a businessman in 1955. During that time, Senator Thurmond also offered her a position in his practice in Edgefield, but she declined it because she married the businessman and moved to Allendale.

Eva initially joined the firm with G. H. Kearse and then opened a solo practice. She found herself juggling the demands at the office with the responsibilities of raising four children. In the effort to better manage her time, she accepted the position of town clerk in 1964. Ten years later, Eva re-established her solo office, became a licensed real estate broker, and served several terms in the Allendale town council. For the last five or six years of her active practice, Eva represented the Department of Social Services on a contract basis in the family court of Allendale.

Eva is now retired and living in Columbia. "Her door was always open, and I doubt that she ever turned anyone away for an inability to pay. She should be remembered for her compassion and willingness to serve others regardless of their ability to pay her," Barbara Brunson said.

Two of her children, a son and a daughter, became attorneys.

(64) Maxine Scarborough
admitted June 16, 1954
?–1991

While it is unclear why Maxine Scarborough decided in her mid-thirties to study law, as well as why she practiced less than one year once she was licensed, she certainly had ample opportunity to apply her legal education throughout the latter half of her varied career.

Maxine was a coed at the University of South Carolina during the Depression years, graduating in 1937. That year, she was maid of honor in the May Court. She was an attractive undergraduate student who drove a Packard convertible that was golden brown like the color of her hair. She did not want for beaus.

In the 1940s, Maxine joined the graduate history program at Columbia University in New York City, where she received a master of arts degree in June 1947. A few years later, she tried to enroll in law school at her alma mater in Columbia, but was denied because classes had already begun for that semester. She promptly applied to George Washington University in Washington, D.C., where she was given an entrance exam and admitted. She received her bachelor of laws degree from that institution on June 1, 1951.

For less than twelve months, Maxine kept a law office open on Main Street in North. "She never did say why she went to law school," recalls Edwina B. Kennedy, one of her daughters. Maxine lived most of her life in the five-bath, eleven-room house on Palmetto Drive in North. She knew the famous singer Eartha Kitt and her family, who lived out on the road to Orangeburg. The house became known as the Scarborough House, although she inherited it through her maternal grandparents. Maxine also inherited a cotton gin, a store, and about one thousand acres outside of North where she raised cotton and beans. She transacted all her business on the telephone from the den of Scarborough House. "Things like tracking commodities and playing the stock market were her business," explains Kennedy.

During this time, she also learned to pilot an airplane, buying a third interest in one.

In the early 1960s, her mother, father, sister, and two grandparents all died within one year. Then, her brother, David Edgar Scarborough, filed a lawsuit against her seeking construction of the will of their maternal grandfather. At issue was a fee simple, conditional estate relating to a portion of the one thousand acres. The decision of the state's Supreme Court in this case is of record in *Scarborough v. Scarborough,* 246 SC 51, 142 S.E. (2) 706 (1965). In this case and subsequent litigation between the parties, Maxine was represented by Columbia attorney Augustus T. (Clint) Graydon.

The year the case was decided by the Supreme Court, Maxine became a single parent, adopting a newborn baby girl. The following year, she adopted another baby girl. Both adoptions were through private placement without the assistance of an adoption agency.

In the second action of *Scarborough v. Scarborough* before the Supreme Court, the court recognized her right to sell timber off land over which she had a fee simple title. Both of her daughters believe these lawsuits were of great import in her life and understood that she even gave legal assistance to the cases in her own behalf. The second case was reported in *Scarborough v. Scarborough*, 249 SC 331, 154 S.E (2) 110 (1967).

During the time her daughters were students in the public school system, Maxine served two terms on the North School District Board.

Since Maxine Scarborough's death in 1991, stories about this charismatic woman have become legendary in North.

(65) Ruth Williams
admitted December 14, 1954 (The author)
1928–

Every September at Winthrop, when I was a student there in the late 1940s, President Henry R. Sims would pontificate to the all-female audience, "For the hand that rocks the cradle is the hand that rules the world."

It never occurred to Sims that I might want to rock the world! It was in a constitutional law class, taught by the case method, when I realized I wanted go to law school. I went to law school because I saw the legal profession as being the center of power. My goal as a lawyer was to be able to tap into a touch of clout and to hover on the periphery of the movers and shakers.

When I stood before the Supreme Court taking the oath to become an attorney, I was among the last neophytes to swear not to settle disputes by dueling. I have kept that oath.

Between my second and third year in law school, I asked the president of the Charleston Bar, Robert Figg, if I could work for him without gratuity. In his office, I prepared memorandums of legal research. I would read sitting on one side of a tall bookcase and listen to Figg and Thurgood Marshall talking on the other side. As opposing attorneys, they were preparing for the most significant litigation of their careers, *Briggs v. Elliott*, the school segregation case.

Figg never assigned me to do research for this case. Most of the discourse I overheard between Figg and Marshall was not about the segregation case; it was easygoing banter between two colleagues.

I resumed my research work for Figg after I finished law school. As he began to close his law practice to assume the position of dean of the law school, I learned to check titles to real estate. Attorney Joe Cabaniss then offered me a free desk in the office of Hope and Cabaniss, and I relocated there. Other lawyers became my clients as I checked their real estate titles. Joe took me to my first annual meeting of the local bar. I did not know until I arrived that I was the first female to attend, and I did not know until almost fifty years later that a senior member objected to my presence. The Charleston women lawyers who preceded me had never attended this annual meeting.

After checking thousands of titles and changing law offices several times, I had earned enough money to buy a Volkswagen and a little, old Charleston house. From 1962 through 1964, I served one term in the state's House of Representatives. My experience in politics was beneficial in my law practice. When I represented clients before boards, commissions, or other political bodies, it helped my clients when my name and face were recognized.

What was then one of the largest law firms in the state, Sinkler, Gibbs, and Simons, asked me to become an associate to manage their real estate department. I consider my experience in this firm to be of major significance to my professional career. Working daily from 8 A.M. to 6 P.M., chasing paper at the office a half day on Saturdays, being alert at early Tuesday morning office meetings, I felt some of the prestige of the firm touch me. Office meetings began with someone briefing the most current court decisions, followed by disclosure and discussion of some contentious ongoing litigation in the firm's trial section, and closed with office-housekeeping details. My monthly financial draw and my year-end bonus calculated by the percent my department brought in to the firm led me to fancy that I was the highest paid woman lawyer in the state.

In the late 1960s, this firm represented the Medical University of South Carolina. When the university president asked my managing partners if he could offer me a position on his staff, they agreed. I was not eager to make this move and bargained to maintain a small private practice as well. Once I was ensconced in a grand office near the president, I realized there really was not much legal work to do in-house at this institution. In the mid-1970s, the president terminated my position.

At age forty-five, I married and joined that small cadre of lawyers who were wedded to physicians. Our group used to laugh together and say, "We are the lawyers who can really screw the doctors."

When I re-entered practice, I realized that young women around me were pursuing all fields of the legal profession. They had opened every professional door for me! Starting a new practice in 1975, I calculated that out of every one hundred dollars I earned, forty dollars of it went for overhead, thirty-five dollars was paid in taxes, and I found only twenty-five dollars in my purse. Nevertheless, I relished the small cases (e.g., the dog bite case in the Friday night magistrate's court). Between 1990 and 1994, I served as associate probate judge of Charleston County, a part-time position. Now that I am in my seventh decade, avoiding cases fraught with stress, I am aware that an antique gun for hire will not realize the financial rewards today's models can command. For me, however, hovering on the periphery is still an exciting pursuit. Looking at my professional biography from the present viewpoint, I know I would not have joined an organization of women lawyers in the 1950s—there was none. I just wanted to blend in with other members of the bar.

(66) Mildred T. Griffin
admitted December 14, 1955

In the 1950s, Mildred Griffin, a 1926 graduate of George Washington Law School, moved to Beaufort where a cousin lived. She was accompanying her ailing husband, who was relocated from the Naval Hospital in Honolulu to the Parris Island facility at her request. Some members of the Beaufort Bar report that Griffin was the first woman assistant district attorney in Hawaii.

After being admitted to this state's bar, Griffin accepted a position with the Dowling Firm, checking titles to real estate. Later, she established her own law office at 819 Bay Street, but continued to specialize in title examinations. Her husband died while in the Naval Hospital, and Griffin continued her practice in Beaufort until the mid-1960s. According to her friends in Beaufort, she was living in St. Petersburg, Florida, in 1973. She is now deceased.

(67) Louise Boucher
admitted June 15, 1956

The *Greenville City Directory* from 1955 through 1957 identify Louise and Ernest W. Boucher as living at 10 Brooksdale Drive, Apartment 3-B, and Ernest W. Boucher as being a member of the United States Air Force. Betty Dendy of the firm of Haynsworth, Perry, Bryant, Marion, and Johnson recalls that Louise Boucher was associated with that firm during the mid-1950s. "She worked in the real estate department and her husband was a pilot stationed at Donaldson Air Force Base in Greenville."

(68) Winifred G. Wills
admitted December 14, 1956

Now retired in her hometown of Monetta, Winifred Wills James said that many years ago, "My teenagers asked me, 'Mamma, why don't you practice law and buy us a Porsche?'" She explained, "The year after I was admitted, I married Marshall James, an Episcopal priest, and chose to stay home with my children over practicing law, but I have had some remarkable encounters in the legal profession." Actually, even as a child, Winifred was well acquainted with the legal profession, having Judge Steve C. Griffith and attorneys Jeff and Joe Griffith as uncles.

When Wills enrolled at Furman, her father told her she had to get a teacher or secretary certificate. She chose the latter, combining it with a major in political science. Her political science courses included constitutional law taught by the case method used in law schools. (This course has influenced other women in this study, as noted, to choose law school.) An extracurricular event of profound significance that Wills attended in 1947 was South Carolina's famous last lynching trial.

After graduation from Furman and a year of graduate school in political science at Louisiana State University, Wills became a secretary at the law firm of Leatherwood, Walker, Todd, and Mann in Greenville. While there, she shared a house with four other women, one of whom was Jackie Rainwater, admitted in 1949, who was then working in the office of John Bolt Culbertson. Wills, of course, had observed Culbertson in action during the lynching trial.

D. B. Leatherwood encouraged Wills to go to law school, so she enrolled at the university in the last class that could elect to graduate in two years by taking three semesters each year. She chose the two-year course. After admission to the bar, she returned to the Leatherwood firm. Although a neophyte, she argued a case before the state Supreme Court during her first and only year with the firm. She had a unique qualification he hoped would sway the court.

The facts of the case centered around a client who brought some liquor for sale into the state from North Carolina without paying this state's stamp tax. "Mr. Leatherwood asked me to make the oral argument in the Supreme Court because he knew all the justices were aware that I had married a man of the cloth. The chief justice greeted me in open court. Even that didn't help the facts because the court ruled against us."

While her husband, the Reverend Marshall O. James, served a congregation in Jackson, Mississippi, the senior warden of the church, an attorney, encouraged her to take a position in his law firm. "I lasted one week. I wanted to be home with my children." While in that state, James got the necessary ticket to witness the second murder trial of the man charged with killing Medgar Evers, the Civil Rights leader, yet another "remarkable encounter" in the legal profession.

When James and her family moved back to South Carolina, she contacted the bar association about "renewing" her license to practice law and was told that she did not have to take the bar examination again, but must pay the license fee and take the required continuing legal education courses. James still opted not to practice law although she got all the qualifications.

"None out of three children followed in either of our professional steps," James said.

(69) Etta Mathe Morrison
admitted December 14, 1956

The Columbia office of the United States Internal Revenue Service employed Etta Morrison during the mid-1950s. The city directories for the years 1953 through 1958 identified Morrison's home as being at 221½ Harden Street, Columbia. There is no further information about Morrison in subsequent directories.

(70) Suzanne Blackwell
admitted December 14, 1956

The community of Hodges in Greenwood County was home to Suzanne Blackwell at the time she was admitted to the South Carolina Bar. On the day after her admission, *The Greenwood Index-Journal* published a story announcing that twenty-one persons had been admitted to the bar, including a "Negro woman, Suzanne Blackwell of Hodges."

Senior United States District Judge Matthew J. Perry, Jr., says that "Having never met Ms. Blackwell, I do recall that for a brief period following her admission to practice law in South Carolina, her certificate as a licensed attorney was displayed in the office of Harold Boulware of Columbia. Mr. Boulware later became a family court judge in Richland County. . . . I recall having been told that Ms. Blackwell was admitted to the practice in another state and that she had not attended law school in South Carolina."

On December 19, 1929, Blackwell purchased her first piece of real estate in Greenwood County. Her deed described the property as twelve acres in the Township of Cokesbury. In February 1975, she executed a conveyance of some real estate in South Carolina. Her residence then was in Washington, D.C. She is listed in Washington telephone books in the 1960s and 1970s as "Suzanne Blackwell, N.P.

1752 S. NW Number 7." The initials probably stand for "Notary Public." In the directory for 1971, Ms. Blackwell is listed in the yellow pages as an attorney, giving her office address as that of her home. There is no estate of record in Greenwood County for Ms. Blackwell.

She was the second African-American woman lawyer admitted to the bar of this state.

(71) Betty Jo Edens
admitted August 2, 1957

At Edens Plaza Shopping Center on Columbia's West Beltline Boulevard Center are the offices of The Jebco Corporation, Mid-South Investment Company, Blythe Investors, and a parking space labeled "Reserved for B. J. Edens."

Edens says:

What I really hoped to do with my life was to become a psychiatrist and/or clinical psychologist. I double majored in English and psychology in undergraduate school, but somehow got diverted to law school. When I first entered, I did not intend to go the full three years and finish, but somehow along the way, I changed my mind. But it was not because I had a burning desire to be a lawyer. I was a member of the honor society, Wig and Robe, and on the editorial board of the Law Review.

When I finished law school, my father asked that I help him in his manufacturing business, which fabricated custom-made signs and skylights. (Mid-South Industries, Inc.) I went with the intention of helping out during the summer months, and remained because I felt needed. I was offered a job by one of the prominent law firms in Columbia, but a prerequisite was that I type all my own documents. I was not a proficient typist and had always had someone else type my papers in undergraduate school as well as graduate school. It would have taken me forever to type a lengthy document, and I would have had a nervous breakdown worrying about the errors in it.

A current brochure of Mid-South Industries, Inc., describes Edens in this fashion: "She obtained a bachelor of arts degree in the

School of Arts and Sciences at the University of South Carolina, after which she completed her studies in the School of Law. . . . Her wise counsel and advice in handling legal matters, including lease and conditional sales contracts for the company, have been of inestimable value. Her capable and efficient management of financial affairs for the company have been a substantial factor in the successful development of Mid-South."

Edens remained in this position for about ten years. "Thereafter, I began to assist in the management and development of family-owned real estate companies in which I was a partner and have been involved in this endeavor to the present time. Needless to say, my legal education was beneficial and useful in both instances. But the actual legal work constituted only a small portion of my time, the bulk of which was spent handling various other duties and responsibilities. I am about ready to retire, although I'm still actively engaged in managing my real estate companies." Edens adds with a smile, "And I am still a frustrated psychiatrist."

(72) Virginia Aiken Gaston
admitted July 2, 1958

Virginia (Gina) Gaston Hennig mastered some legal terms when she was still in diapers and first learning to talk. As far back as she can remember, her circuit judge grandfather, her attorney father, and all the visiting judges to Chester would gather at their family dinner table and discuss the litigations of the day. Even now, legal subjects are still passed around her table among four lawyers—Gina, her husband, son, and son-in-law.

When Gina graduated from Converse College with a degree in English and chemistry, she was unsure of what she would do next. Her father suggested that she go to law school in Columbia. "He was the greatest influence on me," says Gina, "but I did work for one year in New York after graduating from Converse. When my father and I went to the law school at the university, we had an interview with Dean Samuel L. Prince, who said to me right in front of my father, 'Why do you want to come down here and bother all my boys?'"

Gina was named for her grandmother, Virginia Carolina Aiken Gaston, and Gina has a copy of her grandmother's 1898 Greenwood High School graduation speech in which she made a singularly prophetic statement, "One day, women will be lawyers and other professionals and wear pants!"

Upon admission to this state's bar, Gina joined her father's law firm in Chester. In that practice, she did some criminal defense work in the general sessions court making plea bargains, but not trying cases, the same with Driving-Under-the-Influence clients in the local police court, and she checked a few titles to real estate.

Three years into the practice, she married a Yale Law School graduate, Julian Hennig, who joined his father in the family business of August Kohn Mortgage Company. While Gina did not actively practice law after she was married, her professional training contributed to her understanding and maintaining an interest in the activity of her husband's mortgage loan company. Occasionally, she has checked titles of real estate in Charleston for the August Kohn Mortgage Company, and when she goes home to Chester, "I join in the legalese talk at the dinner table."

(73) Jean Agnew Galloway
admitted July 22, 1958
?–1990

The Jean Galloway Bissell award is the highest honor that can be bestowed on a woman attorney by the South Carolina Women Lawyers Association. This prestigious distinction is given in Bissell's memory annually to one who "Influences, opens doors, and advances opportunities for women in the law."

Jean Galloway Bissell was the first South Carolina woman to serve as a federal judge. At the time of her appointment, she was professionally associated with the South Carolina National Bank and the highest-ranking woman banker in the United States.

She was born in the small town of Due West, which was built around Erskine College, where she began her college education. Her undergraduate and law degrees were magna cum laude, and she was elected to Phi Beta Kappa at the University of South Carolina. The psychologist who interviewed Jean when she was being hired by the bank said of her ". . . dismissing comments about her many academic and professional achievements by saying that all the Galloway women were highly educated and successful . . . it was the men who didn't have the advantages. They were expected to go to work in the textile mill as soon as they could."

Her classmate, Virginia Gaston Hennig, remembers that upon Galloway's admission to the bar, Jean accepted a position as an assistant to the first woman admitted to this state's bar, James M. Perry, admitted in 1918, at the Greenville law firm of Haynsworth, Perry, Bryant, Marion, and Townsend. Six years later, she became associated with the Columbia law firm of McKay, Sherrill, Walker, Townsend, and Wilkins.

In 1976, Galloway Bissell assumed the position of general counsel and senior vice president at the South Carolina National Bank, and in the following year, she became its executive vice president. A year later, she was appointed vice chairman and chief administrative officer, a position she held until she was nominated to the bench in 1980. At her congressional judiciary committee hearings, she was asked how her work at the bank prepared her for a position on the federal bench. She replied, "As chief legal officer for a multimillion dollar corporation, I have had sole final responsibility for the legal matters, including litigation, for these past years. This, therefore, has made me intimately aware of the judicial system and the absolute need on the part of the parties involved in litigation for the expedient, efficient administration of justice. This is an absolute necessity for all parties."

Beginning in 1968, she served on the Daniel Foundation, the charitable organization of the Daniel International Corporation, an engineering and construction company. At her memorial service on May 8, 1990, a former chairman of that company recalled that before she joined the court, Jean requested that a major donation be made to the National Center for State Courts in Williamsburg, Virginia. "Jean was instrumental in every grant the Foundation ever made to education." He added that she sometimes represented the corporation "and not only was she a superb lawyer, but, in the vernacular of the construction business, she was tough and she knew how to operate."

One of her many pro bono services was as chairman of the University of South Carolina Law School's board from 1979 to 1982.

Her appointment to the bench was upon the nomination of U.S. Senator Strom Thurmond. The appeals court to which President Reagan appointed her is a special appeals court with national jurisdiction for limited federal legislation subject matters, such as, but not limited to, patent and trademark issues. The judiciaries of this court are identified as circuit judges.

At her judiciary committee confirmation hearings, she was asked what actions she would take as a judge to ensure that the court is current while it maintains judicial quality. Bissell answered, "You do that by working until the backlog is reduced. I think in my history of twenty-five years in the practice of law and working, I have never had more than two weeks vacation in any one year, and in the last eighteen months, I have not had a day of vacation due to the fact that a job needed to be done and I am willing to do it. . . . In addition to this, my husband says I am a workaholic."

The *Almanac of the Federal Judiciary* (1989) Volume 2 cites *Coplin v. United States,* 761 F2d 688 (1985) as one of her noteworthy rulings. Briefing this case, it states: "The Federal Circuit reversed the Claims Court and held that the Panama Canal Treaty, and its related Agreement, does not exempt U.S. citizens who are employees of the Panama Canal Commission from payment of U.S. income taxes on income derived from their work for the Commission. Rather, it exempts them only from payment of Panamanian taxes. The Supreme Court affirmed, *O'Connor v. United States*, No. 85-158, 55 U.S.L.W. 4007 (11-4-86)."

In that same *Almanac* report, lawyers' evaluation of Judge Bissell were cited and some specific comments were:

> *Probably the hardest working judge on the court; has read everything on case-briefs, records, relevant law.*

Her questions get to the heart of the issues.

She is very serious about what she does.

I would call her a 'plugger'. If there is a loophole, she will fill it. If you go from A to C and miss B, she will probe how you got there.

Opinions are solid. They get to the heart of the issues.

Smart, able.

I think she is still learning the law in the government contracts areas.

Good business background, knows tax law, works hard.

After Judge Bissell died of cancer in 1990, a colleague, Judge Helen Neis, commented at the memorial service on Bissell's craft of drawing orders, "She feared writing broadly, that is, more than necessary for the decision in the case because it might unwittingly prejudice the next litigant or worse, jiggle something on a wholly different point of which she was unaware. Her opinions became models of succinctness, accuracy, and precision."

One of her former law clerks gave this eulogy at her memorial service:

She and her husband, Gregg, included her clerks, interns, staff, and their respective loved ones as part of the judge's own family. The family feeling helped to induce a high level of personal commitment to the judge and it spawned high levels of productivity. . . . She was a voracious reader and virtually inhaled written material.

At that service, her brother and fellow attorney remarked, "She certainly felt that she was at no disadvantage because she was a woman and so those that encouraged her saw none either."

It may seem ironic that Judge Bissell allegedly was not in favor of joining an organization composed exclusively of women lawyers, yet her name is attached to the highest award given by the South Carolina Women Lawyers Association. Her point of view needs to be evaluated in terms of the climate of her times, when being accepted on an equal footing with men was the primary goal. To achieve this, Portias of her day may not have had to masquerade as did the original, but they certainly needed to appear asexual. By the last decade of the twentieth century, it had become safe and acceptable for a woman attorney to be her whole self—female, intelligent, and "lawyerly." An award in Bissell's name is a tribute to her efforts to make this possible.

Milly S. Dufour, 1951.

Irene G. Krugman, 1952.

Eva R. Hightower, 1952.

Maxine Scarborough, 1954.

Ruth Williams, 1954.

Winifred G. Wills, 1956.

Betty Jo Edens, 1957.

Virginia A. Gaston, 1958.

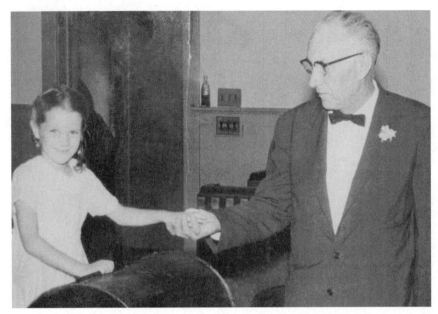

Jury Girl Pamela Hughes and Clerk Lloyd Fleming, 1954.

Nicholas Wilson and Fanny Britton Wilson, 1959.

~ Six ~

Women on the Edge

Throughout the 1960s, the nation experienced cultural convulsions. There was the Civil Rights Act of 1964, the Civil Rights Movement, the Vietnam War, the anti-war demonstrations, the marketing of the birth control pill, the striving for the Age of Aquarius, the growing sexual freedom, and the surge of the second wave of feminism. Despite tumultuous societal changes and legal reforms in this decade, not until the end of the 1960s was there a discernible impact on women in the legal profession in South Carolina. There were, however, valiant and successful efforts to modernize state law.

The long-range effects of the 1954 *Brown v. Board of Education* decision, culminating in the Civil Rights Act of 1964, slowly, but inevitably, made themselves felt in South Carolina. Ernest F. "Fritz" Hollings, an attorney, was governor in 1963 when he admonished the General Assembly that its separate but equal position regarding state education had come to an end. There were not going to be any further lawsuits. He declared that South Carolina had no further courts of appeal. "This General Assembly must make clear, South Carolina's choice, a government of law rather than a government of men." African-American students were admitted to the university in Columbia the following school term.

The law school in Orangeburg closed after the spring semester of 1966, and its students enrolled at the law school at the university.

It is noteworthy that there were no women listed on the roster of the law school alumni of Orangeburg's South Carolina State College. In the college yearbook of 1963, *The Bulldog*, there is a picture of Laura Ponds of Camden as a first-year law student. In the 1965 yearbook, Laura Ponds is shown as a senior in the law school. At that time, she identified New York City as her home. Laura Ponds was not admitted to the practice of law in this state.

Racially desegregated education in South Carolina by no means automatically desegregated other public facilities. In 1968, I witnessed a clot of some thirty-five African-American young men and women as they marched through every hall on all three floors of the Charleston courthouse. When they walked out of the building, the "colored" signs on bathroom doors and water fountains had disappeared. Bystanders made no protest, and the signs were never replaced. National and local demonstrations supporting desegregation pockmarked the 1960s, contributing to the general unrest.

A trenchant factor enabling women of all races to enter the work force was the marketing of the birth control pill in the early 1960s. This landmark step toward sexual freedom enabled women to plan ahead to prevent conception without requiring medical intervention, such as the Intrauterine Device (IUD). While other means, such as the diaphragm, had been available to women, use was not recommended until shortly before the act of intercourse, an unreliable time for exercising precaution.

The United States Supreme Court issued a decision regarding birth control. The opinion, though not a trailblazer, was at least an acknowledgement of the right to choose. In the case of *Griswold v. Connecticut* 381 U.S. 479 (1965), the court concurred in recognizing that married couples can use birth control. The issue arose out of the conviction of a medical director and an executive director of a Planned Parenthood League as accessories for giving married persons medical advice on the prevention of conception and prescribing a device or material for that purpose. Connecticut had a statute making the use of contraceptives a crime and permitting the prosecution of anyone who assisted another to commit this offense. The United States Supreme Court held that this statute violated the rights of marital privacy, which are within the penumbra of specific guarantees of the Bill of Rights.

Greater sexual freedom notwithstanding, anguish brought by desegregation and the civic turbulence created by anti-Vietnam War protests figured large on the national stage. Meanwhile, South Carolina struggled to bring itself into the second half of the twentieth century. The issue of allowing women to serve on juries was considered and defeated by each General Assembly from 1949 until 1966. Then the necessary legislation to permit the electorate to approve a constitutional amendment was prodded by a federal court decision pertinent in Alabama. I was a member of the 95th General Assembly in 1963 and 1964 and recall that at the time, there was no expectation of sufficient votes for passage. (Allegedly, the major objection was the cost to provide jury lavatories, two for males and two for women, one each for "Coloreds" and "Whites.") I concluded that the reason for the defeat of this measure was that the plaintiff's attorneys controlled the House and Senate. They did not want women on their juries because they assumed women could not think in terms of big money (i.e., large verdicts).

In April 1980, Arnold Shankman wrote an article on this subject published in the *S.C. Historical Magazine* and said:

> *In 1965, Heyward Belser of Richland County, chairman of the House judiciary committee, spearheaded a movement to grant the women their due. Most of his colleagues agreed and rejected the argument of attorney and Representative Fred Buzhardt, who warned that it would be "tragic" if white women had to serve on a jury with black males "who might not be so desirable." On April 15, 1965, the House voted sixty-eight to eight to submit a referendum to the voters at the next general election. . . . There was no victory celebration. (Without two-thirds vote of both branches of the legislature.) Thirteen days later, Attorneys McGee (Joseph H.) and Belser arranged for another vote (but it failed too).*

On February 7, 1966, before the next session of the legislature could consider the matter, a three-judge federal district court in Montgomery, Alabama ruled in the case of White vs. Crook that Alabama's statutory exclusion of women from jury service was an unconstitutional violation of the equal protection clause of the Fourteenth Amendment.

The decision was not completely unexpected in South Carolina as Representative Belser had long maintained that there was a substantial possibility federal courts could reverse the conviction of women criminals if it could be demonstrated that females were systematically excluded from juries.

In the Senate debate, the chairman of the judiciary committee argued that he did not want women to serve on juries with illiterates; therefore, a bill was passed to require jurors to have at least a sixth-grade education. On November 8, 1966, sixty percent of the voters endorsed the amendment. The constitution was amended to read:

All persons charged with an offense shall have the right to demand a trial by jury. The jury in cases of civil or criminal in all municipal courts, and courts inferior to Circuit Courts, shall consist of six. The grand jury of each county shall consist of twelve persons, all of whom must agree to a verdict in order to render the same. Each juror must be a qualified elector under the provision of this Constitution, between the ages of twenty-one and sixty-five years, and of good moral character.

The act was ratified March 1, 1967, and women's names were added to jury pools that week in some counties, but this was not uniformly applied throughout the state. It took about twenty-four months to be fully implemented. Joe Cabaniss, a Charleston defense attorney, said, "Before women were admitted to the jury, we had only white males on the jury. I used to look over the jury and count those with neckties. If my jury had seven neckties, I knew I had a defense jury; less than seven ties, it was a plaintiff's jury."

Another anachronism in South Carolina legal practice that was eliminated in the late 1960s was "trial by ambush." Prior to 1968, the state court rules pertaining to discovery of the adversary's position were very limited, permitting stunning the opposing attorney with surprise evidence and witnesses. After 1968, the state Supreme Court started adopting and phasing in federal rules, including taking depositions. Needless to say, these procedures can make it very expensive for a plaintiff to prepare for trial (e.g., in January 2001 in Charleston County, a patient in a medical malpractice action had to spend $120,000 to prepare for his day in court).

Attorney J. Lawrence Duffy believes these high costs have contributed to the growth in the number of big law firms and the resultant fewer "boutique" partnerships. Clientele of large firms generally can look to their defense clients to advance funds for discovery. A senior partner of a firm large enough to have offices in Europe, Atlanta, Georgia, and five South Carolina cities told me that when discovery rules were set in motion, his "firm started getting tons of paperwork, which had to be read and understood. We hired many paralegals for the document review. This is a task that is tedious and tiresome. We began to replace paralegals with new lawyers, mostly women lawyers. The clients wanted lawyers to do the document review. Women are supposed to be good at detail." A. Arthur Rosenblum, a Charleston litigator, said, "Discovery more than quadrupled the work of legal preparation of a case for trial."

Early in the use of discovery, Sam Craven, a solo law practitioner, was served with ten interrogatory questions on a case he had against J. Rutledge Young of the multiple attorney law firm Young, Clement, Rivers, and Tisdale. Months went by and Craven didn't answer the interrogatories. When their paths crossed, Rutledge would ask him when answers could be expected. Finally, Craven asked Rutledge if he had a book on interrogatories in his office that his secretary could copy. "Certainly, she can come any time," said Rutledge. Craven's secretary, who was also his wife, spent three days copying out of that book. (This was before copy machines.) The following week, Craven served Rutledge with one hundred interrogatories.

Updating South Carolina law and legal practice was capped off in 1969, when as a "housekeeping" gesture, the state finally ratified the Nineteenth Amendment to the United States Constitution, fifty years after Congress had given women the right to vote. "I've been waiting for fifty years to tell you boys what I think of you," said eighty-five-year-old Eulalie Chafee Salley as she chastised the state Legislature for its tardy passage of the amendment. Salley was the wife and mother of two Aiken attorneys, both named Julian Salley. She had persuaded her county senator, who was not a lawyer, to sponsor this bill. Salley's exuberant reaction to the national ratification of this amendment in 1920 was described in an earlier chapter.

Although change came more gradually in the Palmetto State than elsewhere, by the end of the 1960s, about half the women in America held jobs, as did almost half of the mothers of school-age children. Virginia lawyer and congressman Howard W. Smith offered an amendment to the Civil Rights Act of 1964 to prohibit discrimination in employment on the basis of sex. Smith never revealed whether he hoped his amendment would defeat the Civil Rights Act or if he expected it would fight sexual discrimination. In any event, his amendment to the Civil Rights Act passed and went into effect in 1965, one year after it was passed.

A working mother was the major "new woman" of the decade, so was the educated daughter. The number of women admitted to the professional ranks began a steady rise.

The first time the bar examination was given in 1960 was the final opportunity to qualify for this exam by "reading law," the term for studying law under the tutelage of a member of the bar to qualify to take the bar exam. In the 1950s, as discussed in the previous chapter, the South Carolina Legislature gave the Supreme Court the power to set the prerequisites for admission to the practice of law. The court changed its Rule 5, limiting the admission to those who graduated from law school. A provision was added to accommodate those persons who at that time had already commenced the study of law under the direction of a member of the bar. Both women qualifying in this category passed the bar examination.

(74) Frances Drake Staples
admitted April 15, 1960
?–1990

Frances Drake Staples had a distinguished career in the federal judiciary in this state, starting fortuitously when she went to work at age sixteen as secretary of Cecil Wyche of the Spartanburg firm of Brynes, Wyche, and Nichols. By the time Wyche was appointed to the federal bench in January 1942, Frances Drake had married textile engineer George W. Staples of Spartanburg. She continued as Wyche's secretary.

Staples's friend, Frances Smith, clerk of the South Carolina Supreme Court, relates that Frances Staples enrolled in the LaSalle Law School correspondence course, but always gave credit for passing the bar examination to the preparation given her by Wyche and Assistant District Attorney Arthur G. Howe. "The judge wanted Frances to become an attorney so that she would qualify as law clerk and draw the commensurate salary. She was already doing the work of a law clerk," says Howe. "She drew Judge Wyche's orders. She was his law clerk, secretary, and court administrator."

During the years that Staples worked for Judge Wyche, Donald Russell became associated with the Wyche firm. After Wyche's death in 1967, Staples became the law clerk, secretary, and court administrator for Judge Donald Russell. When Russell was elevated to the Fourth Circuit of Appeals, she went with him, serving on his staff until her death in 1990.

"No one was more adored and respected in the federal court system than Frances," says Howe.

(75) Esther Archer Jones
admitted April 15, 1960

Esther Archer Jones "read law" in preparation for the bar exam in 1960, as a private law student of Professor Charles Elliott, a Columbia attorney and member of the law school faculty, who had also prepared Louise B. Wideman, admitted in 1945. While a high school student, Esther Archer went to work for professor Elliott, who trained her to be his legal secretary. This involved learning how to draft pleadings, use the code, file papers, and eventually help others who were reading law while working in Elliott's office—all this before she, herself, stood the bar exam.

Frances Smith, former clerk of the Supreme Court, remembers Professor Elliott saying, "The summer I went to Europe, I made more money than I ever had before and that was because Esther Archer took care of my office. This was before she was admitted to the bar!"

Although she married Caldwell Jones in mid-life, she remained in the employ of Professor Elliott until his retirement in 1964. That year, she accepted a position in the trust department of the South Carolina National bank, where she was responsible for the bank's estate work. She wrote to Sarah Glymph Wilcox, admitted in 1936, "The work is interesting and heavy. We were totally understaffed when I first went to the bank and we still need help. We have to use a secretarial pool and this is not the best arrangement in the world, but I can see lots of improvements in our efficiency since my short tenure of three years. There is much to be done."

In the late 1970s, Esther Jones became associated with the Columbia law firm of Griffin, Mays, Foster, and Kittrell. While making a career as a behind-the-scenes lawyer, one of the great pleasures in Esther Jones's life was observing the success of other women attorneys.

(76) Angela Mallory Roddey
admitted July 28, 1960

"When I graduated, I wanted to teach in a law school, and there was one woman with tenure in a law school in the United States, Sonia Menchikoff, who had been at the University of Chicago and who had just gone as dean to the University of Miami. Academic law was much harder to get into than law firms," stated Angela Roddey.

"I had fairly realistic expectations of the practice of law when I finished law school. My father, my maternal grandfather, and an uncle all were practicing attorneys, so I knew what it was about," Roddey said.

She graduated from the National Cathedral School in Washington D.C., Newcomb College, and the law school at Tulane University. Since she was too young to be admitted to the Tulane University Law School when she applied, she took her first year at King's College, London, Faculty of Laws.

While Roddey was a student at King's College, she occasionally telephoned Bob Carpenter, the junior member of her father's Rock Hill law firm of Roddey, Sumwalt, and Carpenter, to ask him to help research a point of law. "I couldn't imagine that our firm had a law library as good as King's College," says Carpenter.

Roddey changed her name to Holder by marriage while living in New Orleans. She achieved her coveted position in academia fourteen years after graduation from Tulane, when she became a graduate tutor in instruction at Yale Law School. Prior to going to Yale, she worked in the criminal division of the New Orleans Legal Aid Bureau. Later, she was associated with her father's law firm, and from 1964 to 1974, she taught political science at Winthrop College.

From 1977 to 1989, she was counsel for medicolegal affairs at Yale, New Haven Hospital, and Yale University School of Medicine. Since 1983, Holder has been clinical professor of pediatric (law) at Yale University School of Medicine. Like most successful academicians, Holder has an impressive curriculum vitae—it is twenty-six pages. She has written three books and another is in progress. A list of her publications covers nineteen pages.

(77) Ann B. Morrison
admitted August 10, 1961

"I would give the same advice in the practice of law as in a chess game—go after their weakest position and don't worry about your strengths or weakness. It works both in law and in chess," claims chess professor, Ann Morrison, who teaches in the Atlanta School for Chess, where her son is the chief executive officer. This school maintains an enrollment capacity of 1,200 with about an equal number of male and female students.

For ten years before her retirement on December 31, 2001, Morrison was student service program coordinator on the staff of the academic dean of the University of South Carolina Law School. She assisted the dean with registration, materials, and class scheduling, as well as helping to hire about fifty law students to work for the professors on the faculty and processing their payroll. In addition, Morrison taught an undergraduate class of pre-law students, where she stressed the importance of "critical thinking." Each semester, those classes had a full enrollment of twenty-five with almost as many female students as male.

Justin A. Bridges, Morrison's father, was a law student at the same university in the late 1940s, when she was still in grammar school. At that early age, she told him that she, too, was going to law school, and he was thrilled. By the time she was twelve years old, she was stopping by her father's office in Laurens, where he would instruct her to read certain case files. Then, they would discuss the facts and issues.

Ann Morrison now uses her legal education as a professor of chess. It was a successful transition.

(78) Patsy A. Fortinberry
admitted August 10, 1961

Patsy Fortinberry presently lives in McComb, Mississippi, and continues an active membership in the South Carolina Bar Association. She is a graduate of the law school at the University of South Carolina. Fortinberry did not respond to me after receiving a certified letter with receipt returned requesting updated information.

(79) Miriam F. Britt
admitted August 6, 1962

Miriam Britt Benjus is now a lawyer in Connecticut, where she and her husband "have a busy little law practice."

She learned to brief law cases in undergraduate school at the university in constitutional and international law classes. "When I graduated from law school at the University of South Carolina, I was not confident, and I thought, 'Nobody would expect anything from me. What am I going to do with my life?' I went home to Georgetown unemployed. An attorney named King told me that God revealed to him that I was going to take over his office when he died. I tried, but decided, 'This is not for me.'"

In January 1963, with no prospects for a job, Britt caught the overnight train to Washington, D.C., to look for a position. "I just walked up and down those broad avenues looking at federal buildings and deciding which ones to walk into and ask for employment. Within two weeks, I had a position in the office of the general counsel of the Department of Housing (HUD). I stayed there about eight and half years when I switched to the Veterans' Administration. Then I met this guy with an odd last name, Benjus, and married him."

The couple later moved to Michigan, where they were involved in matters relating to that state's Uniform Relocation Act. Eventually, they settled in Stamford, Connecticut, where they have an active law office. She concentrates on probate cases, and he maintains a large group of real estate clients.

(80) Betty Sue McBride Sloan
admitted August 19, 1963
1923–2000

Betty Sue Sloan was known to have the chutzpah that most women lawyers need. She is believed to be the first woman in this state to wear pants in the courtroom. Her practice was primarily criminal defense work "because she loved to defend the bad guys," says her retired Marine Corps colonel husband, who was proud of his wife.

For her sixteenth birthday, Sloan's father gave her flying lessons. World War II interrupted her education at Converse College, and she returned home to Alabama to graduate from college and to enroll in the aeronautical program at Auburn University. In 1945, she married her six-foot-four-inch Marine. When her husband received a routine military assignment to the University of South Carolina in 1960, she decided to enter law school. At that time, their children were ages thirteen, ten, and six.

Colonel Sloan writes this story: "She was offered a position in a firm in Columbia. She accepted. The first day, a gentleman from the firm handed her a rough draft of a brief—'Betty, run this through the typewriter.' She replied, 'I don't type.' Friday, after a very slow week, Betty asked the gentleman to step to the window overlooking Washington Street. 'Sir, just across the street there the workman is hanging my shingle and my secretary will type that brief for you if you still have it.' Thus, Betty Sue McBride Sloan's law career began—solo—just as her sixteenth birthday began her career in aviation—solo. She enjoyed every day of it."

"Big Red" was how the inmates at the state penitentiary knew Betty Sue Sloan. Her popularity there stemmed from her representation of a prisoner named Mayfield, who was given a life sentence and had served thirty years when Big Red sprung him.

"They were the most interesting clients," she would swear. One of her clients, an escape artist bandit, could not be kept in prison. On one escapade, he got as far as New Mexico and Arizona. Another time, she represented a Latin gentlemen who was incarcerated for stealing construction equipment.

Sloan closed her office in 1993 when she and her husband began extensive holiday traveling. Colonel Sloan reports, "She enjoyed Scotland, the home of her father—the Isle of Skye. She was not known to pass up a taste of single malt."

(81) Ellen Virginia Hines
admitted August 13, 1964
1940–1998

The professional life of Ellen Hines consisted largely of actions creating opportunities for disadvantaged people to get legal services and forging openings for women lawyers to serve as judges and mayors. In addition, she initiated the establishment of a home for troubled adolescent girls, a program for disabled athletes, and two medical clinics for those with no health insurance.

Hines graduated from Agnes Scott College, was second in her class at the university law school, and then joined her father's law practice in Spartanburg. She married D. Lesesne Smith, III, a real estate broker. Just six years later, she was appointed chief judge of the civil and criminal court of Spartanburg County, the first female judge in that county. Thirteen years after being admitted to the bar, Ellen Hines Smith formed the Spartanburg Legal Aid Society, the predecessor of Piedmont Legal Services, Inc. Employed as its executive director for eighteen years, she transformed that agency from a one-room office with one desk and one chair into an organization that served all of western South Carolina. Among other awards, she received the ten-thousand-dollar Kutak-Dodds Prize, a distinction for Legal Aid Service lawyers.

Previously, in 1974, Ellen Hines Smith helped to establish, and then served as its first chairman of the board of directors, the Spartanburg Girls Home. Since her death, it has been renamed in her honor. She also created HALTER, a program to help disabled athletes enjoy horseback riding, and founded two St. Luke's Free Medical Clinics, one that provides services to those with no health insurance and one for migrant workers.

In 1982, Smith became the first woman elected to the Spartanburg City Council, and she was also the first woman elected mayor pro-tem. She was re-elected twice without opposition.

It takes three pages to list all of Ellen Hines Smith's numerous honors and awards, including the South Carolina Women Lawyers Jean Galloway Bissell Award. During her prolific life, she survived two heart attacks and open-heart surgery, dying of cancer in 1998.

(82) Dorothy Vermelle Sampson
admitted August 26, 1964

Dorothy Sampson of Sumter graduated from North Carolina Central University law school in Durham. After her admission, she opened an office at 39 South Washington Street, Sumter, with her twin brother, Donald Sampson. He was admitted to the bar in June 15, 1951, and also maintained a law practice in Greenville. Problems arose in Dorothy Sampson's practice in the late 1960s, and on November 15, 1982, she was indefinitely suspended from practicing law. Although she is entitled to apply for reinstatement of her license, she has not done so.

(83) Nancy Catherine McCoy
admitted August 30, 1966

Nancy Catherine McCoy Waller is senior attorney at the office of Social Security Hearings and Appeals in their Charleston office. Her married name is Waller. Her responsibilities include drawing court orders, advising judges, and passing judgment on Social Security claims that could be reversed on their written records. Waller has been associated with this office for twenty years. Prior to that time, she was a rating board specialist at the Veterans' Administration. She explains, "My office was where the application process began."

At the time Waller was admitted to the bar, she was a resident of Anderson. Her first professional position was as a trust officer for Wachovia Bank in Winston-Salem, where her duties included the management of trust funds for some of the world's largest tobacco companies.

Waller's undergraduate education was at Agnes Scott College. During her three years in law school, Waller was the "recent decisions" editor of the *Law Review* and taught legal writing to the neophyte members of the *Law Review*.

Waller's brother, J. D. McCoy, is assistant United States attorney for this state located in the Greenville division.

(84) Anne Allen Waters
admitted August 30, 1966

Anne Waters Westbrook is an administrative judge in the United States Department of Agriculture Board of Contract Appeals in Washington, D.C. She graduated from the University of South

Carolina Law School in the same class as Nancy McCoy, and they were admitted to the bar during the same ceremony. "My expectations of the legal profession? No doubt, I was influenced by a romanticized memory of my attorney grandfather who died when I was a small child. He had quite a varied practice in Atlanta from 1914 to 1947. Also, as a college senior, I decided to go for another degree, either a master's in political science or a law degree. My major professor advised that the law degree was the more versatile of the two degrees. I'm quite sure that I had little expectation of the realities of the practice."

Waters was admitted to the Georgia Bar a year after her admission in this state, and then for two years practiced in a small general firm in Atlanta. "When I moved to Savannah, I went to work for the Corps of Engineers and there developed an expertise in the area of federal government contracts. That work equipped me for my current position.

"The Agriculture Board is one of the several agency boards on contract appeals that adjudicate disputes between federal government agencies and entities with which they contract. The jurisdiction of the boards is pursuant to the Contract Dispute Act of 1978 and is concurrent with the jurisdiction of the Court of Federal Claims at the election of the contractor. Appeal is to the Court of Appeals for the federal circuit. The Agriculture Board also has regulatory jurisdiction to decide disputes between the Federal Crop Insurance Corporation and reinsured companies which sell multiple crop insurance under the Federal Crop Insurance Act," explains Westbrook.

While in Georgia, Waters married and had two daughters. She added, "As my daughters were growing up, neither evidenced even a remote interest in the law. That changed when the younger was a college senior. After working two years as a legal assistant to test her inclination, she went to law school at the University of Georgia. She is now practicing with an insurance defense firm in Cobb County, Georgia. She is getting good experience—on her third day with this firm, she went to court."

"I freely confess that, with one exception," she said without explaining her one exception, "my career developed as it developed, rather than according to a great scheme of my own. I can also confirm that I have few regrets."

(85) Helen Ehrhardt Clawson
admitted April 13, 1967

"I'm glad I've lived long enough to see mediation. The law is not serving families well, and that is why mediation works," says Helen Ehrhardt Clawson, who has been a part-time mediator since 1987 and a part-time magistrate since 1981. "I did not fit well in the adversary system. My practice is limited to arbitration, mediation, construction contracts, securities, and insurance disputes."

"Deciding to go to law school was a casual decision. I thought, 'My father is a lawyer, I'm his first born, so I'll go to law school,'" says Clawson. While in law school at the university in Columbia, she married classmate Bob Clawson. In her third year, she commuted from his hometown in Hartsville to the law school while serving on the *Law Review* staff, holding the position of chief justice of Wig and Robe, and then graduating cum laude. Asked about her expectations of the legal profession, she replied, "It never crossed my mind that I'd ever work a sixty-hour week.

"My first position out of law school was in my father's office, and when my first child was born in 1971, I considered myself lucky because I could work part time and was in charge of my own schedule," Clawson observed.

Professionally, Clawson is approved by the American Arbitration Association and since 1992, she has served on the South Carolina Supreme Court's commission on Alternate Disputes Resolution (mediation sub-committee).

(86) Martha Garrison Williams
admitted April 13, 1967

Since 1982, Martha Williams has been vice president and general counsel for the Liberty Corporation, based in Greenville. In 1968, when she first became a staff attorney for this public company, the firm was then primarily in the life and health insurance business. Having divested these properties, it now owns and operates a group of network television stations and related media properties. Williams is a member of the American Society of Corporate Secretaries and the American Counsel Association.

Before she was admitted to the bar, Martha Garrison married law school classmate Ray R. Williams, Jr., now a Greenville attorney in private practice. During their first year out of law school, 1967– 1968, U.S. Army Captain Ray Williams was stationed at the Pentagon, and his wife accepted a position as an attorney in the Office of the General Counsel of the U.S. Department of Agriculture. Of that period, Williams comments, "The current events of the late '60s created a tipping point in the lives of most young adults. It was a particularly exciting time to be in Washington."

(87) Mary Jo Sottile
admitted April 13, 1967

Mary Jo Sottile's legal career has been in Washington, D.C., "working on the hill" the first thirteen years.

J. C. Long, a prominent member of the Charleston Bar, was Sottile's cousin. He gave her summer jobs when she was a law student and retained her to do legal research while she was in law school at the University of South Carolina. J. C. Long even gave her her first case after she was admitted to the bar.

As an undergraduate political science major at Hood College in Maryland, Sottile's professor, also a lawyer, influenced her to go to law school. "Cousin J. C. Long couldn't imagine why I wanted to go be an attorney as opposed to getting married." Sottile, Helen Ehrhardt, and Martha Garrison Williams shared an apartment while they were in law school before Ehrhardt's marriage to Bob Clawson.

After her admission to the bar, Sottile became the first female law clerk to the South Carolina Supreme Court, assigned to Associate Justice James M. Brailsford. From this position, she went to the nation's capital in 1968 with an appointment from Congressman Mendel Davis as counsel to the Committee on Armed Services. Her next post was in the Department of Justice as a congressional liaison. In 1974, she became chief legislative assistant for Senator Ernest F. Hollings. While in this office, she married and changed her name to Manning. From 1976 to 1981, she was communications counsel to the Senate Committee on Commerce, Science, and Transportation.

Leaving public service, Manning joined a private Washington law firm, which specialized in matters relating to telecommunications. Presently, she is with the firm of Wiley, Rein, and Fielding. "In Washington, we don't practice law in the traditional way. I do policy advocacy analysis," she states. Her professional publications include being editor of *Technology Policy Update* as well as being a contributing editor of *Transition Report*. In addition to being a member of bar associations, Manning is affiliated with numerous technology organizations.

In response to an inquiry seeking interest and professional biographical information for this state's history on women lawyers, Manning said, "I am not interested and I just put all those questionnaires in the trash."

(88) Barbara Caroline Babb
admitted October 3, 1968

Barbara Babb decided to go to law school while serving as legal secretary to her attorney father, Thomas Babb of Fountain Inn in Greenville County. The first year after Babb was admitted to the bar, she served as secretary to the president of the South Carolina Bar Association, John McKee Spratt. Although their offices were in the Supreme Court building in Columbia, Babb drove to work daily from Fountain Inn, at least an hour and a half one way. Currently, Babb practices law out of her Fountain Inn home at 407 South Main Street.

(89) Kay Frances Paschal
admitted October 3, 1968

Kay Paschal now primarily maintains a real estate law practice out of her home on Kitty Hawk Drive in West Columbia. "When she was first admitted to the bar, she accepted an appointment as counsel to the Commission on Aging," says her law school classmate, the Honorable Thomas L. Houston, Jr. Paschal is the daughter of the late Gary Paschal, Columbia attorney. She did not respond to any inquiry from me.

(90) Jean Hoefer Toal
admitted October 3, 1968
1943–

Taking a course in constitutional law taught by the case method for a mere two weeks convinced Agnes Scott College student Jean Hoefer that she wanted to be an attorney. Since making that decision, her career has been so distinguished that law school professor W. Lewis Burke observed, "You cannot write about Justice Toal. Her contributions are so great that no one can write about her for fifty years." Despite that admonition, I presume merely to highlight a few significant events in the life of South Carolina's first woman chief justice.

Early in life, Toal had a perception of her future as a professional watching her Aunt Salley juggle a career, marriage, and motherhood. Her own mother was a housewife and her father was the owner of a firm that processed and sold sand. However, her parents were delighted when she told them she wanted to go to law school. Her accomplishments in undergraduate school as a debater, a member of the judicial council, and the holder of a Phi Beta Kappa key, prepared her well.

At the University of South Carolina Law School, Toal moved into positions of leadership and academic achievement including, among others, Mortar Board, Order of the Coif, and the editorial staff of the *Law Review*. During her second year in law school, she married classmate William Thomas Toal.

Upon graduation, the couple accepted positions in Greenville, where Toal became an associate with the Haynsworth, Perry, Bryant, Marion, and Johnstone firm. While there, she assisted Jean Galloway Bissell, admitted in 1958, who became her mentor. Bissell was then a specialist in pension and profit-sharing plans for large corporations.

Women being allowed to serve on juries created a significant steppingstone in Toal's career. She explains, "Women's names were not put in the jury pool in Greenville until the court terms of 1968 and 1969. Because so many men had job-related exemptions and women did not, many juries were all female. The trial lawyers in the Haynsworth firm came to me and said, 'You are going to do trial work. Somebody has to communicate with these women.'" Jean Toal began to try cases, and she loved it.

In 1970, Toal became an associate, and later a partner, in the Columbia firm of Belser, Barwick, Ravenel, Toal, and Bender. This firm primarily handles a variety of defense work. "As I developed my own clientele," says Toal, "I expanded our base to include more plaintiffs' cases, administrative law cases, domestic litigation, and employment cases." When she was twenty-eight years old, Toal argued her first case before the Fourth Circuit Court of Appeals. During the early seventies, she won many significant cases, not the least of which, from the standpoint of the woman lawyer, was when she represented law student Victoria Eslinger, admitted in 1974, in her action to accept an appointment as page in the South Carolina Senate. A discussion of that case will appear in the following chapter.

For thirteen years until her election by the General Assembly as a justice of the Supreme Court on March 17, 1988, Toal represented Richland County in the House of Representatives. She says, "I was generally regarded as an expert on constitutional law and state finances." With that reputation, her service included being chairman of the House Rules Committee and the constitutional law panel of the Judiciary Committee.

Toal's co-chairing the "Jimmy Carter for President" committee in 1976 led to her being approached after his election about a position on the bench. She thought about it and decided she was not ready. The offer triggered her aspirations; however, she leaned neither toward the federal bench nor to the state circuit courts, but rather toward a position as justice on the South Carolina Supreme Court. That goal was achieved in 1988, when she was sworn in as an associate justice. From that time until her elevation to chief justice on March 23, 2000, Toal estimates she wrote 330 opinions, not including those on disciplinary matters or per curium opinions.

Even a brief overview of Justice Toal's eminent career must stress her leitmotif—encouraging other women up the professional ladder.

Addressing women at the College of Charleston on September 2, 2000, she said, "It's awfully easy to pull up the ladder and protect what you have and not reach out to those others who are behind." Jean Toal did not write off her obligation to women attorneys with the Victoria Eslinger case. To this day, she will take time out of her busy schedule to discuss a career concern with a female colleague. Much will be written about Jean Toal in the future. For the young female attorney of today, she is both a paradigm and a practical hands-on supporter.

(91) Mary Jeanas Wiesen-Kosinski
admitted October 17, 1968

Mary Wiesen-Kosinski became a South Carolina lawyer after marrying Professor Leonard Kosinski, Ph.D., and moving to Aiken, where her husband was on the faculty at the University of South Carolina-Aiken. "Mary maintained a solo practice primarily in the fields of domestic relations and Social Security disability. As recently as the end of the twentieth century, she closed her office and retired," says her friend and Aiken attorney, Irene Rudnick. Wiesen-Kosinski is a graduate of the law school at University of Wisconsin. She did not respond to any of my inquiries.

(92) Ann Elizabeth Fleischli
admitted May 13, 1969

"I attended the University of Champaign-Urbana for both my bachelor of arts degree and doctor of laws degree. My husband, George, graduated from the same school a year ahead of me, so we were at the school together for two years. Other than myself, no one in my family has ever been or is now an attorney. My brothers and I were the first in my Norwegian/German family to attend college," says Ann Fleischli. Her husband was an officer in the Air Force Judge

Advocate General's Corps and was stationed at the air base in Charleston when she was admitted to the South Carolina Bar.

While they were located in Charleston, Fleischli took a position with the Neighborhood Legal Services, which was then on Spring Street. She described some of her experiences:

I remember Charleston clearly. The heat in high heels and linen dresses, the freshly caught flounder grilled on the beach, the intense poverty and the pride of those I represented. It was a fast immersion into the injustices of society. I was there during the strike of the African-American hospital workers when there were tanks and armored personnel carriers near our offices. Nothing appeared in the local papers as to the thousands in the streets. When I returned to Illinois, I looked up the New York Times' *account of the battles. They covered it well.*

During the strike, I was called by the Charleston jail to talk to a woman who had been arrested for kicking a national guardsman and refused to give her name or post bail. When I walked into her cell, I was surprised to find her to be in her late sixties, less than my height of five feet, and very arthritic and frail. Her crime had been that she and an elderly black man had been walking after curfew and, when challenged by a national guardsman, she had kicked him in the shins with a cloth-slippered foot. The woman's first name, she told me, was the town in Alaska where she was born. She was a graphic artist working for U.S. Steel, but she had an agreement with them that she could take off to visit tyranny wherever, whenever it reared its head. She had been present at the most violent strikes in the century.

Her refusal to give her name and post bail was a ploy to try to get in the papers. I told her that not only would there be no article on her, there was also no coverage of the roughly ten thousand people parading in the streets. No mention of the overflow church crowd to hear the recently bereaved wife of Martin Luther King. Nada.

She was stunned and I told her she would do more good outside jail. She agreed and gave me the number of her employer in Pittsburgh to get the bail money.

When I bailed her out the next day, I remember the police officer on duty yelling at me as I walked out in my linen suit on that hot day, "Hey," he said, "something's fishy. This guy wants to bail her out, too." He was pointing to a black guy, next in line, holding cash in his hand in small bills. It was weird to him that a black guy would be bailing out a white woman from out of town. Clearly there was a plot afoot.

Since those years in Charleston, Fleischli has had a general practice in Madison, Wisconsin, adjusting her schedule around her two daughters while they were in school. "Since they left home, I have been practicing more environmental law. In addition, I have been an active citizen and am fairly well-known in the community."

(93) Margaret Elizabeth Brown
admitted September 10, 1969

Since 1974, Margaret Brown of Charleston has maintained an active membership in the South Carolina Bar Association, but not an active practice of law. After she graduated from law school at the University of South Carolina, she formed a law partnership with her brother, Frederick, and for a time, they had offices at 126 Meeting Street in Charleston. She did not respond to any of my inquiries.

(94) Meredith Johnson Hayes
admitted September 10, 1969

Meredith Johnson Hayes is now a specialist in estate jewelry, but maintains her license to practice law by taking the required continuing legal education courses. "I keep my license current, just in case I want to get dangerous. Since my daughter is a physician, I take a lot of C.L.E.s in medical malpractice to keep her out of jail."

Fresh out of the University of South Carolina Law School, Hayes worked three years at the Federal Power Commission in Washington D.C., following that with three years in corporate law on the legal staff of Sea Pines Company on Hilton Head. "I put in some eighteen hour days. I worked Saturdays and still felt as if the people didn't pay any attention to me. It was hard work. I wanted to stay at Hilton Head, but the only work for a woman lawyer there was in driving forty miles to Beaufort to check titles to real estate. That's when I quit the practice and moved to Atlanta."

For the last fourteen years, Meredith Hayes has been associated with Richter's of Atlanta, an estate jeweler in Buckhead, an affluent section of the Georgia capital.

(95) Gail Eileen Jordan
admitted September 10, 1969

Gail Jordan has parlayed her legal education to the pinnacle of retirement at age thirty-nine, and she now divides her time between a house on a lake in Columbia and one at an upscale site on Longboat Key in Florida. "It has paid off," she told her mother, Laura Jordan, who had to borrow the money for Gail to attend law school.

Three years after her admission to the bar, Jordan, with a partner, started a real estate development company that became very successful. "I could not have made the strides I have without that law degree," says Jordan. Before she started developing real estate, Jordan held a position as an attorney with what was then the Department of Public Welfare, now known as the Department of Social Services.

"I continue to keep up with my annual requirements to take continuing legal education courses, and I pay my bar associations dues, but I now have stopped working," says Jordan.

(96) Nancy Elizabeth Polatty
admitted September 10, 1969

Nancy Polatty moved to Boulder, Colorado, and by 1975, she had discontinued her membership in this state's bar association. After her admission to the bar, she returned to her home in Greenville, where she first accepted a position with Legal Services Agency and later was staff attorney to a Greenville County Council standing committee.

(97) Mary Galley Sinders
admitted September 10, 1969

"I am proud to have been a pioneer for women lawyers in the Veterans' Administration and also to be able to use my legal background in matters affecting my community and state," says Mary Sinders, now a resident of Waveland, Mississippi.

After graduation from St. Mary's School of Law in San Antonio, Texas, in 1953, Sinders accepted a quasi-legal position as a Veterans' Administration claims examiner in the Chicago regional office. While there, she took that state's bar examination and was admitted to the practice in 1962. Subsequently, she opened a solo practice in DuPage County, Illinois. After closing that office, Sinders moved to Columbia, South Carolina, where she accepted a position with the Veterans' Administration as a claims examiner, eventually becoming the only female supervisor there.

Climbing the career ladder, she transferred to the central office of the Veterans' Administration as a consultant to the Compensation and Pension Service. Her next move in management was to the General Counsel's office as a staff attorney, eventually becoming the director of Regional Veterans' Administration in Louisville, Kentucky—the third woman to serve in this capacity. Sinders's last position with the administration was district counsel for the region including Maryland, Virginia, and West Virginia. "I retired from government service on October 31, 1983, and yes, the date of Halloween was significant because the Veterans' Administration had become so political," Sinders said.

Reflecting to a degree the variety of options available to women attorneys in the sixties, the preceding mini-biographies presage the broad spectrum of legal specialties that the female barrister would enter in the next decade.

Angela M. Roddey, 1960

Miriam F. Britt, 1962.

Betty Sue M. Sloan, 1963.

Ellen Virginia Hines, 1964.

Anne A. Waters, 1966.

Helen Ehrhardt Clawson, 1967.

Kay F. Paschal, 1968.

Jean H. Toal, 1968.

Ann E. Fleischli, 1969.

Gail E. Jordan, 1969.

~ Seven ~

Say, Portia, That Is a Light I See at the End of the Tunnel!

In the aftermath of civil unrest in the 1960s, needed reforms were gradually enacted, absorbed, or accepted, as the case may be, during the next decade in South Carolina. The scope of this final chapter is the early seventies. The closure at 1974 was chosen because these concluding professional biographies are evidence that women lawyers have been incorporated into the legal profession.

The increasing number of female attorneys practiced a heretofore unprecedented variety of specialties: environmental issues, consumer protection, criminal defense, civil litigation, appellant causes—to name a few. Additionally, these women admitted to the bar between 1970 and 1974 were the first to be addressed as "Ms." Nevertheless, there were certain customs that changed while others did not. For example, women appeared before the bar wearing miniskirts, but no females in pants were, for the most part, allowed in the courtroom. It is noteworthy that during this time, the number of women admitted to the bar ran about parallel with the number admitted to the practice of medicine.

I estimate that South Carolina had thirty-three women actually in the practice of law at the beginning of the decade, and thirty were either office lawyers, who became known as "transactional lawyers," or real estate attorneys, earning fees as set by local bar associations. The fee schedule, however, came under the judicial scrutiny of the antitrust activities. The hallowed county and state bar associations with voluntary membership were not exempt.

A class action suit was filed against the Fairfax County Bar Association and the Virginia State Bar alleging that their minimum fee schedule constituted price fixing in violation of the Sherman Act, and asking for injunctive relief and damages from the members. This action, like the first shot at Fort Sumter, was heard around the world, at least the insular world of the legal profession.

Traditionally, many of the South Carolina county bar associations printed minimum fee schedules that were updated and changed from time to time. This practice dates from at least the 1790s. Probably it was a custom of the bar brought from London.

Irvin J. Slotchiver, a Charleston attorney, has preserved his copy of this association's last minimum fee schedule. The wording from its "Foreword" follows:

> *At a meeting of the Charleston County Bar Association held on July 2, 1970, it was resolved by the members present that the within Schedule of Minimum Fees be approved and adopted, effective August 3, 1970. Coming Ball Gibbs, Jr., Secretary.*

This lists fees for sixty-two professional services grouped under the following titles: admiralty, collections, contracts, corporations, criminal law, depositions, domestic relations, estates, general matters, litigation, personal injury claims and actions, and real estate. Examples of fees include:

- Trial of crime involving death penalty: Twelve (12) months earnings, but in no event less than $2,500.
- Drawing simple will: $35. Divorce or annulment, uncontested: $250.

- Litigation of matters in which a fund or property is involved up to $5,000: 20%.
- Personal injury actions, the Plaintiff on contingency: 33⅓%.
- Drawing a simple deed: $35. Drawing a simple Note and Mortgage: $25

These fees were relative to other contemporary expenses (e.g., coffee was 69¢ per pound; 5 pounds of sugar cost 39¢; 25 pounds of grits sold for $1.98; a Hoover vacuum cleaner was $159.95; and Sears sold a 7-horsepower tractor for $388).

Upon notice that the class action had been filed in Fairfax, Virginia, there was a hastily called meeting of the Charleston County Bar Association in early 1972 for the purpose of considering how it would respond to such a legal action. During the ensuing discussion, Harvard-educated attorney Robert Hollings raised the legal theory of "conscious parallelism." He explained that, if after the fee schedule is abolished, it is found that members still appear to be using it, the members of the bar could be individually liable for violating the antitrust act. Whereupon, attorney Gedney H. Howe, Jr., made a motion that the Charleston County Bar Association had never had a minimum fee schedule. Of course, everyone knew the motion was buncombe, but it put a smile on members' faces. All those present seconded Howe's motion, and the president declared that the motion passed unanimously. The meeting adjourned. M. M. (Rusty) Weinberg, Jr., a Sumter attorney, said his bar passed a similar motion.

The Supreme Court of the United States took *certiorari* of the Virginia case, rendering a unanimous opinion against the bar, *Goldfarb et ux v. Virginia State Bar et al*, (1975). The Supreme Court considered the argument that lawyers' minimum fee schedules were exempt from the Sherman Act as they involved a "learned profession." There had been judicial recognition of a limited exclusion of "learned professions" from the scope of the antitrust laws (i.e., not within the terms of "trade and commerce"). Fairfax County also maintained that "competition is inconsistent with the practice of a profession because enhancing profit is not the goal of professional activities."

Chief Justice Warren Burger, writing the opinion of the court, said, " [T]he exchange of such service for money is 'commerce' in the most common use of the word. It is no disparagement of the practice of law as a profession to acknowledge that it has this business aspect."

The issue before the court involved a fee for a real estate title examination. The court found the county bar's minimum fee schedule had created a pricing system, a classic illustration of price fixing. The court further held that neither the nature nor the public service aspect of the professional practice provides sanctuary, and anti-competitive conduct of the lawyers in the state and county bar are within the reach of the Sherman Act. In conclusion, it said:

> The interest of the states in regulating lawyers is especially great since lawyers are essential to the primary government function of administering justice, and have historically been 'officers of the court.'

The decision impacted income from the practice of law. I, then primarily a real estate attorney, became aware that some lawyers, in seeking real estate agents as clients, began charging less than the fees shown on the Charleston Bar schedule. Other lawyers had to follow suit. Soon, clients were calling law offices shopping for lower fees.

By 1970, another distinct area of law, sexual discrimination, was being eroded by state and federal courts. Decisions prohibiting sex-labeling jobs or giving preference to men as executors swept away the traditional objections to the Equal Rights Amendment. Originally, it had been introduced in Congress in 1923 at the time of the first wave of feminism. Prior to the 1970s, it never had a chance of passing; however, in this decade, Michigan attorney and Congresswoman Martha Griffiths reintroduced it.

Both houses of Congress passed the Equal Rights Amendment by large majorities in 1972. The Amendment states:

*Equality of Rights under the law shall not be denied or abridged
by the United States or any state on the basis of sex.*

Twenty-eight states ratified the amendment within the first year
after it passed, but South Carolina was not one of them.

Congresswoman Griffiths initiated annual conferences on
"Women in Law" to create enthusiasm for the passage of the E.R.A.
Law student Vickie Eslinger, admitted in 1974, flew to Texas in 1972
to attend such a national symposium. On her own initiative, she
invited the conference to hold its next annual meeting at the law
school of the University of South Carolina. The invitation was
accepted. Eslinger says, "We had the first one, which was funded in
part by a grant from the Ford Foundation." Eslinger and Darra
Cothran, admitted in 1973, co-chaired the fourth national "Women
in Law" conference held in Columbia March 16–18, 1973. The
agenda was focused on problems facing women attorneys and parties to legal actions. The keynote address was given by
Congresswoman Griffiths, who declared that the passage of the
amendment "created a moral climate for reform." The program
included presentations on women in the welfare system, unions, and
politics; rape, marriage, and divorce; as well as issues confronting
women as litigators. Some three hundred women and law students
attended.

Conveniently, prior to this conference, the university law school
had gradually moved into a new 180,000-square-feet, five-million-
dollar law center. There were only two women's toilet stalls in this
center. However, the female students commandeered one of the faculty lavatories for their use.

During the first four years of the 1970s, Congress passed several
equity laws that have had an impact on the practice of women
lawyers and on the practice of family law (e.g., middle income families were allowed to claim income tax deductions for child care if
both parents worked; employment benefits were extended for married women in federal government jobs and for married women in
the armed forces; and sexual discrimination in medical programs was
prohibited).

An event of significance to women comparable to the granting of suffrage was the Supreme Court's *Roe v. Wade* decision in 1973. Asserting the right of women to have an abortion meant the status of women was no longer restricted by their singular function of child bearing. Laws in most states, including South Carolina, prior to the rendering of this decision, prohibited abortion except for the preservation of the mother's life. As a result, illegal abortion was a thriving business.

Celebrating the advances feminists had made during this era, Helen Reddy wrote a song, "I Am Woman, Hear Me Roar." The record she made sold over one million copies, and while she made no reference to "Portia," her inclusion would have been fitting. Shakespeare's Portia was a quaint anachronism. By the last quarter of the twentieth century, so-called Portias had the acceptance of the bar and a large part of the South Carolina community. Additionally, commentary on the changing times, both in the nation and the state, ascribes the gradual inclusion of women attorneys. Not all the women included have used their legal education to erase overt discrimination, but many choices reflect subtler considerations, such as the way women value their lives and themselves, including complex questions of culture, family, and what success (and power) really means.

Concluding this book are short biographies of the thirty-one women admitted to the South Carolina Bar between 1970 and 1974. Their career choices are varied—some within the legal profession and others not. Knowing something about the struggles, limitations, and achievements of their predecessors engenders admiration for the accomplishments of women in this decade. This concluding chapter describes genuine professional acceptance of which "Miss Jim" Perry and Claudia "Jimmy" Sullivan could only dream of in 1918.

(98) Jeannie Baker McLain
admitted September 25, 1970

"I expected to be able to get a better paying and more interesting job with a law degree than with only an undergraduate degree. That expectation was met. I married a law school classmate, quit practicing after a couple of years to have a baby, and never went back to work," says Jeannie Rubin. She married classmate Hyman S. Rubin of Columbia, and they were admitted to the bar in the same Supreme Court ceremony.

The first year after her admission, Rubin was a law clerk at the Columbia law firm of McKay, McKay, Black, Sherrill, Walker, and Wilkins.

During her second year, she was associated at the Columbia firm of Rogers, McDonald, McKenzie, and Fuller.

(99) Sara Belle Rearden
admitted May 11, 1971

Sara Rearden, now a resident of Washington, D.C., is a senior attorney in the office of the General Counsel of the United States Merit System Protection Board. This board adjudicates employment appeals for a majority of the governmental agencies.

While Rearden was growing up in Edgefield, her father was a leader in the state NAACP. In high school, she became active as a student leader of the same organization. It followed that as an undergraduate at North Carolina A & T University in Greensboro, she participated in the south's first student sit-ins in the 1960s, an experience leading to her meeting the Reverend Martin Luther King. She participated in picketing restaurants in Greensboro and was arrested. Sara, with others, was not confined in a jail, but in a hospital. The very establishment that would not serve the pickets in its restaurant had the contract to provide food at the hospital where the protestors were being held.

While attending law school at Howard University, where Rearden graduated in 1969, one of her professors, Thurgood Marshall, became her mentor.

Rearden taught math in the public schools of Ware Shoals in 1964. In 1965, she moved to Washington, D.C., to take a fellowship under the aegis of the Neighborhood Legal Assistance Office. She became the assistant manager of that operation in 1972. When asked if she might retire to practice law in Edgefield, Rearden said, "There is not enough legal business there. I could possibly practice law in Columbia or Aiken."

In recent years, Rearden has joined the adjunct faculty at George Washington University Law School, teaching "Problems of Civil Rights." She also conducts medical malpractice litigation seminars in the law schools of the Washington area. Active in professional organizations, Rearden serves on the Board of Directors of the Federal Bar and the Board of the D.C. Legal Services. Additionally, she is a representative to the Council of Legal Opportunity of the National Bar and for the past seven years has been a voting delegate at the Judicial Conference of the District of Columbia.

(100) Linda Mabry Little
admitted April 12, 1972

Linda Mabry Little was a member of VISTA (Volunteers in Service of America, known familiarly as the Domestic Peace Corps) and assigned to the Legal Aid Services in Columbia when she passed the South Carolina Bar exam. She had never previously lived in this state. Now practicing as M. Linda Mabry, she is in the law partnership of Mabry and Steele, with offices in the Fulton Federal Building in Macon, Georgia.

Mabry's career has been distinguished by cases to eliminate racial discrimination in the hiring and promotion practices of governmental, political, and public utility organizations, as well as businesses such as the Georgia Kaolin Company and the Insurance Company of North America. She considers cases of this type her area of specialty and writes, "My legal education has allowed me to address significant issues in both civil rights and civil liberties."

(101) Ragna Olausen Henrichs
admitted April 12, 1972

A recognized authority in the area of environmental law, Ragna Henrichs is a partner in the firm of Porter and Hodges, L.L.P. in Houston, Texas. She is a member of The Water and Environment Federation of the American Bar Association Section in

Environment, Energy, and Resources; Texas Bar Association Section on Environmental and Natural Resource Law; and Greater Houston Partnership, Environment Committee, and Houston Bar Association Law Section. Additionally, she is the author of numerous professional articles and speeches on the subject of environmental law.

"My first exposure to this field was actually in South Carolina during my volunteer activities with the Columbia League of Women Voters. As I recall," says Henrichs, "the League was working on voter and public education projects on topics of emerging public interest in the early 1970s. Pollution and stewardship of the nation's natural resources was then such a topic due in part to Rachel Carson's new classic work, *Silent Spring*."

Henrichs graduated from the law school of the University of California at Los Angeles in 1969 and while there, she married a chemist. When her husband was on the faculty of the University of South Carolina, she was admitted to the bar of this state. Since leaving Columbia, Henrichs has practiced environmental law, first in Rochester, New York, and then Houston, Texas. She has maintained an active membership in the South Carolina Bar Association.

"At the outset, I expected that a career in the law would provide an opportunity to shape public policy rather than shaping policy through legislation and government service. However, that opportunity has come through interpretation, client education, and advocacy," says Henrichs.

(102) Margaret Corinne Blanks
admitted September 30, 1972

Corinne Blanks, now Cannon, and her late husband, J. Douglas Cannon, opened their law office and partnership in Clemson in 1977. "Since my husband's death in 1989, I have continued as a solo practitioner, and a majority of my clients are men either associated with Clemson University or in private business," says Blanks.

"I was fortunate in that, when I was in law school (University of South Carolina), I clerked for Legal Services in Columbia for two years and, under the Student Practice Rule, actually handled cases in both the county and family courts. This experience allowed me to get to know both attorneys and judges, who took me under their wings and helped in a job search as well as the 'how to' of practice," Blanks states. In the first five years after her admission to the bar, she was associated with the Columbia firm of Kohn and Finkel, where she handled the firm's trial work in small counties, and she observes that she never experienced any problems of acceptance as an attorney.

"At the time I began, being a 'conniving lawyer' was not something a 'nice girl' did. I grew up in a family of very strong women where my grandmother, Cora R. Weir, taught me that I could do anything in life and that I was the only one who could hold me back. I also came of age in the 1960s when women were forging into areas that had previously been dominated by men. I entered law school with a positive attitude and the expectations that I would obtain my goal and begin an active small firm practice after graduation. All of my expectations of the practice of law have been met. It's just as my grandmother taught me. You can do anything you want so long as you work hard, are honest in what you do, and treat others as you wish to be treated," Blanks concluded.

(103) Evelyn Marie Angeletti
admitted September 30, 1972

The point when individuals who enter the legal profession begin to think like lawyers—or more precisely, think analytically—is often unknown. However, Evelyn Angeletti, who majored in history at Agnes Scott College, credits the chairman of that department with teaching her to exercise careful judgment and make judicious evaluation. Upon graduation, she enrolled in Emory Law School in Atlanta. Law diploma in hand, Angeletti chose to buck the fashionable tide of young professionals opting to start their careers in Atlanta. Deliberately, she chose to interview for positions outside the penumbra of that current Mecca—the Buckhead section of Atlanta.

This decision led to Angeletti accepting a position with the Greenville Haynsworth firm. She describes herself then as a "baby

Haynsworth lawyer." By 1977, she was ready for a move and joined
Martha Garrison Williams, admitted in 1967, as a staff attorney at the
Liberty Corporation. They were associated for thirteen years and for
a time were the only two women attorneys in Greenville.

From the Liberty Corporation, Angeletti opened her own office
for the solo practice of law on East Washington Street in Greenville.
Over a decade later, her practice is focused primarily on commercial
and residential real estate or other business-related matters.

(104) Patricia O'Dell Brehmer
admitted September 30, 1972

After graduation from law school at the University of South
Carolina and upon her admission to the bar, Patricia Brehmer took
a position as an associate in the office of the attorney general of the
state. By 1977, the *Charleston City Directory* records her last name as
Pearson and notes she was on the staff of the Neighborhood Legal
Association in Charleston. The following year, Pearson was associated with attorney Gary Lamberson in his office on Cosgrove Avenue
in North Charleston. After that date, her professional association is
not noted in the *Charleston City Directory* or *Columbia City Directory,*
and she did not reply to any request for input into this history.
Presently, Patricia Pearson and her husband live on the Isle of Palms,
and she maintains an active status with the bar association.

(105) Mary Carrington Salley
admitted September 30, 1972

"I can't identify my expectations of the legal profession by lofty
goals. The truth of the matter is that I wanted to be able to support
myself," says Carrington, the name she has used since she was twelve
years old. "My mother always wanted her girls to be educated
because 'you never know if you will have to support yourself.'" Her
mother was a career woman, "an unusual phenomenon in the upper
middle class South Carolina of the fifties. My mother worked when
she was pregnant, she worked when she was nursing, and she worked

on Saturday mornings." Her mother and uncles, including Chief Justice Jean Toal's father, owned a sand mine company.

When Salley graduated from the College of William and Mary with a degree in government, her cousin, Jean Toal, was graduating from law school. "So I figured if Jean can do it, I can, too." After admission to the bar, she was associated with a Columbia law firm, staff counsel to the state House Judiciary Committee, and clinical instructor at the law school.

From 1974 to date, Salley has been a member of the Florence County Bar and presently practices under her married name of Wingard. She has served as a Florence municipal judge and as assistant solicitor of the Twelfth Circuit. Not until May 2000 did she open her own office at 401 West Cheves Street, Florence. "My primary professional identity has been as a prosecutor, and to this point, I have enjoyed that more than any other professional experience." Having hung out her shingle, she reports, "I cannot say business is booming, but I am working steady. I talk with almost everyone who comes through the door, but I find I am concentrating on domestic, criminal, probate and employment matters."

Carrington Wingard is the first woman attorney in this state to be a prosecutor.

(106) Edna Louise Smith
admitted September 30, 1972

Edna Smith, who now uses her married name of Primus, is the managing attorney at the Palmetto Legal Services on Bull Street in Columbia, where she has been a staff attorney since 1980. Prior to that, however, she had been a party to two significant events, the former as a law student and the latter as a litigant in a United States Supreme Court decision setting a precedent in law.

"Regarding my expectations of the legal profession upon being admitted to the bar, I'm not sure I had any of note. I think I just wanted to be licensed and employed. As to my feeling on being the first African-American woman at the University of South Carolina Law School, I didn't know that when I was admitted and paid little attention to it afterwards. My goal was to graduate," says Primus. "There was one overt remark about my going to another school (that happened to be predominately black, but which did not have a law school), but I basically ignored the comment. Perhaps my ingenuous nature controlled/directed my action reactions. Who knows?"

Shortly after graduation, Primus was with a firm where one of the attorneys was a staff council for the ACLU. Through this association, she wrote a letter to a woman indicating the ACLU would like to file a suit for her with regard to a specific grievance. The South Carolina Supreme Court imposed a public reprimand claiming she solicited clients for financial gain. *In Re: Edna Smith Primus*, 436 US 412, 98 S.Ct. 1893. 56 L.Ed.2nd/417 (1978) the U.S. Supreme Court found that, where an attorney communicates an offer of free assistance to a potential litigant, the lawyer was not in violation of the Code of Professional Responsibility for soliciting clients for financial gain. During the first years of her practice, she was also an instructor in law-oriented courses at the University of South Carolina, Columbia College, and Allen University.

"All my legal career, I've wanted to help people navigate through the system," says Primus. Through her office, Palmetto Legal Services, she gives free legal clinics about every other month or upon request. Additionally, she appears regularly on the WQIC-AM radio station program "Urban Scene," where she answers questions to assist listeners with legal problems.

(107) Treva Gay Ashworth
admitted November 3, 1973

Treva Ashworth is deputy attorney general of the civil division of the office of the Attorney General of South Carolina. "My major area of responsibility is in litigation that has arisen out of constitutional and election issues." She is currently supervising fifteen attorneys in the attorney general's office.

In addition to numerous appearances before the state and federal judiciary and the appellant court, Ashworth has made an oral argument before the Supreme Court of the United States, and on four other occasions she has been there in second chair. Many times, she has appeared before the Supreme Court of South Carolina. "I like appellant work. Doing research stimulates my interest in logic, and I like making arguments in appellant courts because I want to hear the questions from the judges."

A member of the last graduating class of the university high school, then an adjunct of the Education Department of the University of South Carolina, Ashworth attended the university for her undergraduate and law school education. Although an English major, she took a course in logic in undergraduate school, which led her to law school and helped her think like a lawyer. While still law students, she and Liz Crum became the first women law clerks in the office of the attorney general. In this capacity, Ashworth and two other clerks wrote a fifty-page police officer's manual that was distributed statewide. "This was before computers," she hastened to add. She has now been in the office of the attorney general for over thirty years.

When Ashworth appeared at the Supreme Court of the United States for her oral argument, it was regarding a case that arose out of Hampton County concerning an election law change. The other side appealed the case to this court because Ashworth had won in the lower court in argument before a three-judge panel. When she arrived at the Supreme Court on the appointed day, she was shown into the office of the clerk, who was to determine that she was wearing the correct apparel for this appearance. She chose to wear a navy blue suit, white blouse, and pearls. The clerk approved.

The Supreme Court justices provide a gift to each attorney who makes an oral argument—a white quill pen. "There is someone who still makes them by hand for the Supreme Court," Ashworth explained. She admits that she was nervous, "right up to the time I arose from my chair to make my argument." After the case had been presented to the court, her father, James Ashworth, picked up her briefcase, took her by the arm, and proudly escorted his daughter down the steps of the Supreme Court. Her mother took a photo of the two of them descending the steps, which is now proudly displayed in Ashworth's office. After the court argument, her parents treated her to dinner at the elegant Mayflower Hotel.

Sometime later, the Supreme Court rendered its opinion in the matter. It was nine to zero for the other side.

(108) Mary Ann Breakfield
admitted November 3, 1973

Mary Breakfield, who now uses her married name of Greenwood, is the human resource officer for the City of Miami Beach, Florida, with responsibilities including labor negotiations and risk management. Actually, her professional life has been in the area of human resource appointments for a decade. Prior to her current position, Mary was with the county attorney's office in Key West, where she had human resource responsibilities.

After she completed her undergraduate work at the New School of Social Research in New York, Greenwood entered law school at the University of Southern California. She was admitted to the bar of this state while her then-husband was a Marine stationed at Parris Island in Beaufort. Shortly after her admission, she was associated with the Beaufort firm of Harvey and Battey.

Beginning in 1975, Greenwood became the in-house attorney at Winthrop University for three years, and subsequently she served in that position at the University of North Carolina-Greensboro and at Colorado College. Much of her career has been in the academic community, where she also acquired a master's degree in English and a master of laws degree from George Washington University. For two years, she was on the faculty of Stetson Law School in Florida.

Greenwood has been admitted to practice in Massachusetts, Colorado, and Florida, as well as maintaining active status with the bar of this state.

(109) Darra Williamson Cothran
admitted November 3, 1973
1948–

Darra Cothran is a partner in the law firm of Woodward, Cothran, and Herndon in Columbia, chairman of the Board of

Directors of Sandhills Bank, and a legislative lobbyist for a national insurance trade association. In reference to the law firm, Darra says, "Ours is a general business practice, and I specialize in government and administrative matters."

Specifically, her practice includes adjudicating regulatory matters, rendering business decisions, and representing utility clients before the South Carolina Public Service Commission. She has been in the private practice since 1978.

This Clemson University cheerleader graduated with honors in biology and three months later, she entered law school at the University of South Carolina. While a law student, Cothran participated in many student associations, including being co-chairwoman of the committee for the Fourth National Conference on Women in Law held in March 1973, described earlier in this chapter.

Upon being admitted to the bar, she became a staff attorney with the Charleston Neighborhood Legal Assistance Program for a year. The next year, she helped set up a similar program in the northern coastal counties, serving as its senior staff attorney.

Cothran enjoys the practice of law, particularly since she has begun to specialize for her business clients. "This allows me to streamline my practice and have more free time for travel and for accepting community responsibilities."

(110) Mary Elizabeth Crum
admitted November 3, 1973

Born in Denmark, Bamberg County, into a family of lawyers, Liz Crum is a graduate of Agnes Scott College and the University of South Carolina Law School. Currently, she is a shareholder in the McNair Law Firm, and is located in their Columbia office. She is in the Administrative and Regulatory Section, having gained extensive experience in government regulations relating to health care.

Crum says, "I represent care providers (i.e., hospitals, physicians, nursing homes) in obtaining regulatory approvals for matters dealing with billing issues, complying with federal anti-kickback and state statutes, health insurance portability, accountability, and all matters relating to contract negotiations." Further, she represents clients seeking to construct wastewater treatment facilities and those seeking approval of the South Carolina Department of Labor, Licensing, and Regulation.

After her admission to the bar, Crum became an assistant attorney general in the attorney general's section of Special Litigation. Following this and before she joined the McNair Firm, she spent four years as staff counsel and director of research for the Judiciary Committee of the South Carolina House of Representatives.

Liz Crum is the only woman attorney in the history of this state who has played a round of golf with a United States Supreme Court justice. On April 5, 2000, Federal Judge Michael D. Duffy asked Crum to join them in a 9:30 A.M. tee-off to play golf with Justice Sandra Day O'Connor and her husband at the Yeamans Hall Club in Charleston. Judge Duffy insisted that Crum share the golf cart with Justice O'Connor, who immediately introduced herself and asked Crum to call her "Sandra." Crum just could not bring herself to call the justice by her given name. "She is absolutely delightful and is a good golfer. I knew it would be a lot of fun, but I was not sure how easy it would be to talk to a justice," she recalls. Actually, they only played thirteen holes before they stopped to join attorney Charlton deSaussure and his wife, Ann, for lunch in the club. That was long enough for Crum to know that the justice is a "ringer."

(111) Joan Karen LeCraft Henderson
admitted November 3, 1973

In 1990, President George Bush elevated Judge Karen Henderson to the United States Court of Appeals for the District of Columbia, replacing Kenneth Starr. Previously, she had been a judge appointed by President Ronald Reagan for the United States District Court of South Carolina, the first woman seated on the federal bench within the state. The appeals court on which she currently sits consists of three judges who hear only oral arguments with no witnesses and no juries.

Henderson, who is from Oberlin, Ohio, chose Duke University for her undergraduate studies and graduated from the University of North Carolina Law School in 1969. She practiced law in Chapel Hill until 1971 when she moved to Columbia with her physician husband. There she accepted a position as assistant attorney general, which she held from 1973 to 1978, followed by appointments as senior assistant attorney general (1978–1982) and deputy attorney general (1982–1983). From that date until she was appointed to the federal bench, Henderson practiced law in the Charleston office of Sinkler, Gibbs, and Simons.

Henderson was given an honorary doctor of laws degree from the University of South Carolina in 1994, and she has been awarded the South Carolina Order of the Palmetto. She maintains two homes, one in Columbia and another in Alexandria, Virginia.

(112) Sandra Marguerite Milner Schraibman
admitted November 3, 1973

Although Sandra Schraibman's mother was a Charlestonian and Schraibman was born in that city, she spent her teenage years in Columbia, where she graduated from Dreher High School. Her father was in the U.S. Army. In 1973, Schraibman graduated from the University of South Carolina Law School and from there, she went to Georgetown University Law Center in Washington, D.C., receiving a master of laws degree in trial advocacy in 1978.

Prior to her present appointment in 1986 as an assistant director of the Federal Programs Branch of the Civil Division of the United States Justice Department, Schraibman worked in the same division, supervising actions filed in the federal district courts.

"One of the most memorable cases during that time period was brought by CNN against the White House to gain access to the press pools that followed the president on his trips. The three major television networks objected to CNN's inclusion in the pool. I spent many hours at meetings in the White House Counsel's office and participated in the preparation and defense. Ultimately, CNN became part of the press pool," Schraibman related. "I also personally handled a challenge to the constitutionality of both houses of Congress having chaplains and starting off each legislative day with a prayer."

For six years before her present appointment, Sandra was an assistant director in the same division, supervising actions filed in the federal district courts.

(113) Kathryn Anne Workman
admitted November 3, 1973

A native of Woodruff in Spartanburg County, Anne Workman is a judge of Superior Court in DeKalb County, Georgia, and has been a member of the judiciary of that county since 1982. The jurisdiction of this Superior Court includes misdemeanor criminal actions and almost all civil actions, regardless of the amount claimed. Judges in Georgia may be appointed by the governor and subsequently elected, or initially elected by a non-partisan vote. She was the first woman magistrate, chief magistrate, and state court judge in that county, which has a population of about six hundred thousand.

After graduating from Emory Law School in 1972, Workman took the Georgia State Bar exam and was admitted. The following year, she accepted a position with the Legal Services Agency in Greenville because her father in Woodruff was in failing health. That year, she took the bar exam of this state and "did not know any of the people sworn in with me in 1973."

Workman's high school education was as a boarding student at the Salem Academy in Winston-Salem, North Carolina. She received her undergraduate degree from Duke University in 1969. "I was a student of Professor Robert Rankin. I took his undergraduate class in constitutional law, which relied on the case method of instruction. I was particularly entranced by the *In Re Gault* decision in our classroom discussion and wanted to pursue work in juvenile law as a career," she said. *In Re Gault,* 387 US 1, was a landmark case holding that an accused juvenile was entitled to legal representation and a judicial hearing. The facts in the case involved a child being "sentenced" by a social worker and a policeman.

"In all candor, I must admit that I went to law school because my father would pay for it; and, because as a history major who could not type and who did not have a teaching certificate, I did not have a lot of career opportunities. I was very lucky; however, once in law school, I found it was something I truly loved," reports Workman.

The year after she was admitted to the bar of this state, Workman returned to DeKalb County as solicitor of its juvenile court, where she served for seven years. Before she became a full-time magistrate in 1983, she was in private practice. Between service as a magistrate and Superior Court judge, Workman was a judge of the State Court from 1985 to 1998.

Anne Workman is a Life Fellow in the Lawyer's Foundation of Georgia, selected for demonstrating outstanding legal abilities and a devotion to community. She was given the Golden Apple Award in 1994 for an elected official's contributions to the cause of mentally retarded citizens.

(114) June Hawker Gorman
admitted November 3, 1973

June Gorman, then a resident of Hilton Head, was the first woman member of that island's bar and the fourth in Beaufort County. Now semi-retired, she lives in Wenham, Massachusetts. The bar of the island alleges she was an attorney-gladiator in the mammoth lawsuit that dismembered Ma Bell. "The truth is," says Gorman, "when I decided to leave Hilton Head, I called New England Telephone Company to ask about a position because once before, I had been on their legal staff. As a result of that call, I accepted a position as one of the attorneys preparing the defense for American Telephone and Telegraph Company in the litigation. The office for the defense was located in Orlando. We were a legal staff of six lawyers with about two or three hundred support people. Our work was centered on depositions and documents review. When the case was fully prepared, the gladiators, who were the trial attorneys representing Ma Bell, tried the case in a Washington, D.C., court."

Graduating from Radcliffe College, Harvard University in 1956 as a chemistry major, Gorman was initially employed by the Shell Development Company. However, she soon decided to go to law school with the ambition of becoming a patent attorney. She graduated in 1961 from Boston University School of Law. Her first legal work was doing title searches for a large law firm, but in 1964, she was appointed a special assistant attorney general by Edward Brooks, and subsequently was hired as a lawyer by New England Telephone and Telegraph Company.

On a cruise, Gorman met the man she would marry. She describes the years 1965 to 1975 as "interim retirement." During that period, among other activities, her husband, Dr. Gorman, worked on the hospital ship *Hope* while she lived in Nicaragua and Sri Lanka (Ceylon). As a volunteer interpreter for medical staff, she also wrote vignettes published in a book called *Hope in Ceylon* prepared by a physician heading that project. Prior to moving to Hilton Head, Gorman lived in Myrtle Beach, where she co-founded and was president of the Montessori Child Development Center that operated between 1969 and 1971.

While living in Hilton Head, Gorman was admitted to the South Carolina Bar, and was associated with the firm of McNair, Brown, and Smoot, but is best known for her work lobbying for the passage of the Equal Rights Amendment. Columbia attorney and state Senator Travis Medlock had been retained to represent Equal Rights America in this state. Medlock sent an airplane to the island to fly Gorman to guest appearances on radio and television, and to speak before community and political groups. On a trip to Boston, she gathered all the support material she needed from Harvard University. The television cameras even followed her to her law firm office to conduct an interview. Gorman writes, "On Woman's Equality Day in the 1970s, the Parris Island Marine Depot awarded me with a citation for the ERA work. That was a proud moment for me."

When asked about her present professional status, Gorman said, "My experience is that, as women lawyers 'season,' it is more difficult for them to obtain permanent legal positions. I have been frequently retained on a contract basis (at good hourly rates) by both temporary law placement agencies (Kelly Staffing has a national, temporary law placement service) and temporary mortgage placement agencies. The mortgage agencies place employees having appropriate skills with banks and mortgage companies. I have frequently audited commercial, construction, and residential loans for banks. This requires a review of legal documents and does not require accounting skills. I have also been assisting the office of the attorney general with opinions and analysis concerning coastal litigation involving beach rights and coastal law issues. Currently, I am exploring a contract opportunity with a public land trust that requires real estate opinions relating to old and complex land titles."

(115) Marylea Walker Byrd
admitted May 15, 1974

Marylea Byrd was suspended from the bar association for non-payment of fees just two years after her admission to the practice of law. In the year she was admitted, Byrd was an attorney with Columbia's HUD office. She and her husband, John W. Byrd, a tax manager, then lived at 1500 Blanding in Columbia. The couple, it may be assumed, left the Columbia area as no further reference to them can be located there.

(116) Helen Page Dees
admitted May 15, 1974
1928–1993

Page Dees was in the solo practice of law in Myrtle Beach from the time she was admitted to the bar until her death from multiple sclerosis in March 1993. Judy Zane, one of her sisters, reports, "I called her Pamela Mason, a feminine name for the television attorney, Perry Mason. She was always in court and represented some pretty tough customers."

Dees worked in New York City after she graduated from Mount Holyoke in Massachusetts, and it was there that she first experienced symptoms of multiple sclerosis. Later, she earned a master's degree in political science from Louisiana State University. Then, Dees entered law school at the University of North Carolina, where she graduated Phi Beta Kappa. She became a member of the South Carolina Bar in order to open a practice in Myrtle Beach where her mother lived. "Our grandfather and two of our uncles were lawyers; our father and another two uncles were physicians, but Page was the first professional woman in our family," says her sister.

(117) Ann Mary Stirling
admitted May 15, 1974

Ann Stirling has the highest rating given by *Martindale-Hubbell Law Directory*, and has been listed in *Best Lawyers in America* since 1994. *Best Lawyers in America* is based on a peer review survey in which attorneys throughout each county rate their colleagues. She is one of the few select members of the American Academy of Matrimonial Lawyers. She hopes to retire from her Charleston office around 2011. Since 1977, she has been in the private practice of law, limiting her caseload exclusively to the family court.

After completing undergraduate studies at the University of North Carolina and earning an honors degree in English and Russian history, Stirling then took the first of several years away from academia. She worked in New York City before entering law school at the university in Columbia. "I was not career directed. I did it just to have something to do," she admitted. While a law student, she took off for a semester, and after graduation, she took off for another year to be the "pest lady" in a Colorado plant shop. During this period of her life, Stirling has written that she was "an ardent acolyte" of the late Jerry Garcia and Ken Kesey. "I devoured *The Electric Kool-Aid Acid Test* by Tom Wolfe." Although she chose not to follow indefinitely the life style of these icons of "pop culture," she writes she will be "eternally grateful" to them.

When she returned to South Carolina, Stirling accepted a position with the Charleston Public Defender's Office. Three years later, she was deputy director of that office, got married, and then began private practice.

"I have spoken at tons of Continuing Legal Education seminars, but I don't like it because I am trying to restrict my life to the environs of Charleston," says Stirling. When asked if she enjoys trying difficult cases she yelled, "No! To settle every case is my goal."

(118) Victoria LaMont Eslinger
admitted June 11, 1974
1948–

Vickie Eslinger was asked to be partner when she joined Nexsen, Pruet, and Pollard, LLC in 1991, and her office is now in that firm's Columbia building. She is listed in *The Best Lawyers in America 2001–2002* for family law. Additionally, for a number of years, Eslinger has been a member of the faculty of the Harvard Law School Intensive Trial Advocacy Course. In her firm, Eslinger says that she specializes in "difficult and complex domestic and personal injury cases, but my most interesting ones are employment related."

Earlier in her career, Eslinger was the defendant's attorney who prevailed in the state Supreme Court decision of *The University of South Carolina v. Wade T. Batson and Paul Blackstock*, 271 SC 242, 246 SC 2d 882 (1978). "The effect of this decision was to keep Frank McGuire as basketball coach at the university," she says. At that time, McGuire was an icon of college basketball coaches. The university's arena was named for him. The issue in that case was based on the trustees' policy that mandated faculty retirement at age sixty-five, although there was a contravening state statute setting mandatory retirement at age seventy.

Vickie Eslinger is the daughter of Vassar Eslinger, who was admitted to the bar a year after she was born. Her father and some of his fellow law students would play poker at his home on the nights he had to baby-sit. One of the poker-playing law students was Joe Cabaniss, who now says he thinks baby Vickie must have been listening to their talk about law school and the law.

Beginning in 1964, this Columbia resident took her undergraduate and law school education at the university. "It was a time of turmoil and protests," Eslinger remembers, "but it was also a time when women were beginning to be taken seriously." She admits to being a "rabble-rouser, but it was in that atmosphere that I went from being a Goldwater Girl in 1964 to suing the state, so I cannot say they (the university) trampled on my will. I have to say they shaped my experience. It was a good place for a strong woman."

During her first year in law school, she organized twenty-four volunteers to answer a hot line for abortion advice, a time when legal abortions were not available in this state. This organization operated on zero budget. She was also in demand as a speaker for women's rights.

In that same school year of 1971-1972, the clerk of the state Senate refused to honor her senatorial appointment as a page. With the then-attorney Jean Toal and two lawyers from the American Civil Liberties Union, she filed a sexual discrimination case against the Senate and the state. Two years later, her plea prevailed on appeal. When asked if she felt any repercussions from the law school because of the lawsuit, Eslinger answered, "Only one—my favorite professor, Coleman Karesh, would call me Page Eslinger."

In the same school year that she filed the sexual discrimination suit, Eslinger flew to Texas to attend a Women in Law conference and, while there, invited that body to hold its next annual meeting at her law school. The invitation was accepted, and the fourth annual National Conference on Women and the Law (as noted earlier) was held at the university in March 1973.

After Eslinger's admission to the bar, she formed a partnership with a law school classmate, Madelyn Drake Bourgeois, and then with Lucy Knowles and Ann Furr. In 1976, Eslinger, Knowles, and Furr wrote a thirty-six-page booklet titled *Current South Carolina Laws and Procedures Which Are Sex Biased.* This was a report for the South Carolina Commission on Women. The following year, Eslinger and Knowles wrote a forty-three-page booklet titled *The Legal Status of Homemakers in South Carolina.* It was prepared under contract with The Center for Women Policy Studies of Washington, D.C., where Michigan attorney Martha Griffiths was chair. Both of these booklets are filed in the Thomas Cooper Library of the university.

In 1981, Eslinger accepted a position in the Paris office of the American law firm O'Malveny and Myers, which was then located at 3 Rue Royale above the famous five-star Maxim's restaurant. Her fluency in French, Spanish, and Italian was an asset. Of her year in Paris, she remembers, "I would just throw back my head and cackle to think that little Vickie from Columbia was walking to work in such an elegant city." It was while she was in Europe that she met and married another American expatriate, Rick Creswick, a theoretical physicist.

When the couple returned to Columbia in 1984, she became associated with the law firm of Berry, Diokar, and Jerdon. The following year, Eslinger's name was included as one of the partners. It was from this law firm that she was recruited by Nexsen, Pruet, Jacobs, and Pollard, LLC, to be a contract partner with them. Of her present law partnership, Eslinger says, "I will be here 'til I die."

(119) Judith Louise Bourne
admitted August 21, 1974

Judith Bourne has been in the solo practice of law in St. Thomas, U.S. Virgin Islands, since 1982. Her practice focuses on litigation of all kinds in the territorial courts, with a significant portion of it in the family division. She reports that mediation is gaining strong support there. A distinctive feature of the practice is that the judicial system has only one suzerain because the government of that territory is a creature of the United States Congress.

Bourne majored in English, getting an undergraduate degree from Cornell University in 1966. She graduated from New York University with her doctor of laws degree in 1972 and a master of laws international degree in 1974. During the summer after her second year in law school, she accepted a position to study the loss of land ownership in this state by African-Americans. Bourne was one of six students in the program, each assigned to a different southern site. Her work was done at Penn Center, Beaufort County. Their research was published in a book by Robert Brown titled *Only Six Million Acres.*

After her legal education was completed, Bourne wanted to return to the south and chose Charleston. "New York is an impossible place to live," she says. "I preferred the more sedate life style as opposed to the congestion and hurried place of high density."

Bourne did not have the one-year residency requirement when she was ready to take the South Carolina Bar exam. Attorney Ray F. McClain filed a petition on her behalf with the bar examiners, challenging that requirement. The case was resolved when she was allowed to take the bar exam within the year, but not admitted to the bar until the end of the year. In 1974, Bourne was the only African-American woman lawyer in Charleston, and she estimated that, at that time, there were only six hundred in the United States. "I practiced law in Charleston with Bernard Fielding, Armand Derfner, Charles B. Bryan, Jr., and McClain. I was there for four years, and I felt myself putting down roots. I knew I had to make a decision about staying. I decided I wanted to get into litigation."

That choice led her to accept a position as a federal public defender in St. Croix and St. Thomas, the U.S. Virgin Islands, where Bourne's parents had West Indian roots. She was an attorney in that public defender's office four years before opening her private practice on the island. Bourne is listed in *Who's Who in American Law.*

(120) Constance Beth Ackerman
admitted November 14, 1974

After three years in the practice of law, Connie Ackerman did not renew her membership in the bar association. Identifying the reason for her frustration with the law, Ackerman says, "When I was representing a father, I lost a custody case and decided that the law is spastic. I decided that I'd tote bricks before I'd continue to practice law."

Ackerman graduated from Smith College in Massachusetts. "There we were trained to be an overachiever," she says. "My dad ran for mayor of Charleston and got defeated, and that is when I decided I needed a legal education and went to the University of South Carolina Law School.

"Suzie Ravenel and I graduated together and for three years, we worked for my dad. Our pay was about the same as what was paid at the Legal Aid Society. We had fun and then we quit at the same time."

(121) Madelyn Drake Bourgeois
admitted November 14, 1974

Madelyn Bourgeois Butts, now living in Greer, is using her legal education to further her genealogy research and writing. Actually, she has always been intrigued by the stories of the past and was an undergraduate history major at Furman.

Trying to get a job after college, she was asked, "How fast can you type?" Her stepfather, Philip Wittenberg, was an attorney, and she concedes he probably influenced her to go to law school. "Actually, I never thought I would practice," says Butts. However, she notes with considerable pride that she is a descendent of Winnsboro attorney James H. Rion, the president of the state bar association in 1886.

After her graduation from law school at the University of South Carolina, Butts (her married name) and classmate Vickie Eslinger practiced law together in Columbia for about a year and a half. Then she joined Wittenberg's Florence firm, which did a lot of commercial law and bankruptcy cases, but no criminal law. "I hated it. I am a people person," she says. Presently, she is surrounded by a host of ancestors speaking to her through their legal documents and family histories.

(122) Karen Bulmer Cassidy
admitted November 14, 1974

When Karen Bulmer of Wenatchee, Washington, decided to attend law school, she was attracted to the University of South

Carolina. The propinquity of relatives in Greenville may have been an influencing factor. While a law student, she married classmate James H. Cassidy, now a Greenville attorney. Within a year of their admission to the bar, Karen Cassidy moved to Seattle, Washington. Classmate Connie Ackerman and former husband, Jim Cassidy, believe that she became a member of the Seattle judiciary. I have not been able to confirm that.

The South Carolina Bar Association records show that Karen Cassidy's membership was suspended in 1978 for "nonpayment of dues."

(123) Dorothy Ann Manigault
admitted November 14, 1974

Dorothy Manigault was the first woman attorney from Berkeley County, but she states, "I have never had an office in Moncks Corner, although I have done some practice in the area."

Manigault graduated from the public schools of Berkeley County and attended the University of South Carolina for both her undergraduate and law degrees. Her undergraduate major was journalism, specifically news and editorial writing.

Explaining why she studied law, Manigault observed that she perceived injustices toward minorities in Moncks Corner. She felt the arrest of young black males sometimes seemed unfair, especially since they had no one to represent them in the legal system. Often their families could not afford to hire someone, nor did they trust local attorneys to provide fair treatment. As an attorney, she felt she could assist persons in such situations to ensure they received proper criminal and civil representations.

While a law student, Manigault clerked in the office of Attorney General Daniel McLeod. After graduation, she clerked for I. S. Leavy Johnson, Esquire, of Columbia, and then joined the solicitor's staff under Solicitor James Anders. She migrated upstate with an appointment as executive director and general counsel of the Legal Services Agency of Western Carolina in Greenville. She explained, "This agency served six counties for indigent persons." Ellen Hines, admitted in 1964, established the network of six agencies in 1977.

Governor Richard W. Riley (1979–1982) of Greenville chose Manigault as his executive assistant for legal affairs (legal counsel) and as a liaison to the attorney general's office and Public Safety Department.

Returning to Greenville after working for the governor, Manigault was associated with the law firm of Sampson and Acker, P.A. In 1986, she began her present solo practice. During the first two years, she did consulting work for the Department of Probation, Parole, and Pardon Services, and the Legal Services Agency of Western Carolina, both in Greenville and in Washington, D.C.

Manigault is in solo practice in Greenville and reports, "I would say that sixty-five percent of my practice is devoted to criminal defense, which includes a contract from the County of Greenville to accept assignments of indigent persons; twenty-five percent of my practice is devoted to church and religious business; and the remaining ten percent is devoted to general practice in the areas of real estate closing, family law, probate matters, and personal injury cases."

(124) Adele Jeffords Pope
admitted November 14, 1974

Adele Pope, a descendant of one of the nineteenth century's leading lawyers, James Henry Hammond, is a certified specialist in estate planning and probate law. Her solo practice, set up as a professional corporation, is located at 1507 Richland Street in Columbia. However, Pope had a previous career. She is bilingual in Spanish, having an undergraduate degree from Mary Baldwin in that subject as well as a master of arts in teaching degree from the University of Virginia. Prior to going to law school, she taught Spanish in the late 1960s.

Nevertheless, Pope went to law school at the University of South Carolina and while there, she clerked for lawyers Jean Galloway Bissell and Robert P. Wilkins, distinguished trust and estate attorneys. She acknowledges that when she was exposed to this area of law, "I got hooked." Early in her legal career, she moved into fiduciary litigation and says, "It was a wonderful fit for me." In 1980, she graduated from the University of Miami with a master of laws degree in estate planning.

When she and Thomas H. Pope, Jr., whom Adele Jeffords married during law school, were admitted to the bar, he told her that he would practice in any city where she could get a job. She applied all over South Carolina, but only got a couple of interviews. Then her husband joined his family firm in Newberry, and she took a position in the trust department of a bank in Columbia. While she was working at the bank, attorney Julius W. McKay asked her to join his firm. She admitted to him that she was pregnant, and McKay replied, "I'll go back and ask the firm if it's okay." For most of her professional life prior to opening her solo practice, Pope worked in association with Jay McKay in Columbia. Throughout this time, she has lived in Newberry and commuted to Columbia.

One of the early will litigation cases Pope tried arose in Kingstree. The deceased stated in her will that she "did not have any relatives and didn't want any." Pope successfully represented the relatives, who then lived in Connecticut. The deceased had left her estate to her lawyer, her physician, and her church. "It is a mischaracterization to say that estate litigation is boring."

(125) Suzanne Pendarvis Ravenel
admitted November 14, 1974

Suzy Ravenel is a registered nurse serving in the Intensive Care Unit of the Medical University of South Carolina and has been there since January 1994. "I pay my dues to the bar, but I don't practice," says Ravenel. "I did not like the adversarial system."

"I was influenced by the women's movement that was just beginning when I was at Mary Baldwin College for an undergraduate degree, and it helped me make the decision to go to law school. I was married by the time I began law school at the university, and I took my husband's name as my middle name. Then law students were told that the most valuable course to learn in law school is 'contacts.' Connie Ackerman and I failed 'contact' because we would sit together in the front rows of our classes and 'egg-on' the professor."

After graduation, Ackerman and Ravenel worked in the law office of the former's father, William A. Ackerman of Charleston. This was a disillusioning experience for both young women.

"When I left Bill Ackerman's office, I joined a friend on a sailboat trip to Europe. After I returned, I had three babies and two years later, I tried to practice law out of my house, but I didn't know how to make money. When my brother, William, was a patient in the Intensive Care Unit, I realized that I was comfortable in that setting, and I wanted to be a nurse. I went into nurses training, and I've never looked back," Ravenel said. "Now death is my adversary. As a nurse, I am doing something . . . not just twiddling my thumbs. I'm a visceral individual, a hands-on person."

(126) Sara Ann Sadler Turnipseed
admitted November 14, 1974

For the past five years, Sara Turnipseed has been a partner in the Atlanta office of Columbia's Nelson, Mullins, Riley, and Scarborough, LLP, where she specializes in representing defendants in complex litigation. The largest portion of her work is defending insurance companies in jury trials of asbestos cases. She also represents quite a few defendants involved in environmental and product liability cases.

"During my twenty-seven years of practice, I have also been a government lawyer (United States Environmental Protection Agency), practiced with a small firm, and been a corporation inhouse lawyer (Georgia-Pacific Corporation). I am married to Bill Turnipseed, also a 1974 graduate of the University of South Carolina Law School. He currently has his own law firm, but was with Nelson, Mullins, Riley, and Scarborough for twenty years," explains Turnipseed.

Sadler's parents were the impetus for her to attend law school and to pursue a career as a lawyer. "I am the oldest child in a family of five daughters. My father, a sexist pig at the time, and my mother—a stay-at-home radical feminist in the early 1970s—felt strongly that file clerking, my first job after getting a political science degree from a small Catholic girls' school, Trinity College, lacked adequate intellectual challenge and financial remuneration (eighty dollars a week). I was, quite frankly, nagged to death until I enrolled in law school. They also nagged my sisters, two of whom succumbed and have law or medical degrees. The lawyer-sister, Nancy Doherty Sadler, has her own firm in Beaufort," says Turnipseed.

The Turnipseeds have three daughters who "don't want to be lawyers because they think their parents work too hard. Our older two daughters have chosen marine biology and film/television production for their careers, and our sixteen-year-old wants to rule the world in whatever field provides her the greatest chance of doing so." Sara continues, "I love my life and would change very little of it."

(127) Barbara Mignon Weatherly
admitted November 14, 1974

Barbara Weatherly, formerly of Columbia, is now in a law practice in St. Thomas, U.S. Virgin Islands, centered on real estate and business transactions. Her lawyer associate has substantial business interests on the island. Weatherly believes their sizeable real estate practice stems from stock market money invested in the island.

At the time she graduated from high school in Columbia, her father, Paul Weatherly, "was number two man in the state's technical education system." He then accepted the top position in technical education in the state of Delaware, and Weatherly took her undergraduate college degree in political science at the University of Delaware. She returned to the University of South Carolina to attend law school. "I had wanted to go to law school since I was a little girl. I was interested in politics . . . it was a thrill, an ego boost, especially in South Carolina politics." After she was admitted to the bar of this state, Weatherly taught paralegal students in Dover, Delaware, for twelve years. She had, however, spent many summers in the Virgin Islands, and for this reason, she was attracted to seek her current position. In retrospect, she says, "It's a sacrifice to practice law here because living expenses are so very high. There are a ton of women lawyers practicing in the Virgin Islands, and I wouldn't be surprised to learn that the bar here is fifty percent female."

Perhaps in light of the fact that both her parents were professional educators, Weatherly observes, "I'm not loving the law as much as I thought I would. I'm drawn to the teaching profession."

(128) Sara Marie Walker
admitted November 14, 1974

Sara Walker planned her retirement from the practice of law and then advanced the date a year and a half. Actually, in 1999, she owned her law office building at 1518 Pickens Street in Columbia, but when she had an offer to buy it, this accelerated her retirement plans. Walker retreated to a house and dock on a river near Dreher Island State Park in Newberry County, where she also bought about five hundred acres of farmland.

"There were no lawyers in my family, but I just always wanted to be a lawyer. I loved Perry Mason on television," confesses Walker. She was a literature major as an undergraduate at Queens College in Charlotte. From there, she went to law school at the University of South Carolina, where she was one year behind Vickie Eslinger, who had opened up legislative page positions to women. While a law student, Walker became one of the first pages. "We got paid the same as the boys, but we had some biased rules that they did not apply to the males. If a senator beckoned me over to his desk, it was against the regulations for me to go to his desk, even if he was the one who appointed me."

Upon graduation, Walker worked in the office of attorney Dallas D. Ball for about a year and a half, then went into solo practice. "I started out doing a lot of domestic work, some automobile plaintiff's cases, estate, and drafting wills. I like helping people. Then I got tired of the hassle and retired."

Female barristers, responsible for their actions and deemed peers by their male colleagues, are a reality of the early twenty-first century. This has occurred despite the profession's abiding adherence to precedent, still conspicuous by the fact that only a judge can give consent to set it aside. The accruement of status for women lawyers has come about through small, but steady gains. It is noteworthy that early twentieth century Portias did not have the advantage of women physicians in South Carolina. In October 1894, when this state first required medical licensure, Sarah Allan of Charleston was, without objection, among the initial group.

Although two distinct waves of feminism occurred between 1918, when women were first admitted to the South Carolina Bar, and 1974, the conclusion of this study, it is apparent that personal expectations as well as existing precedents and the socioeconomic milieu affected the women whose short biographical sketches appear in this book. Those who chose to practice law paved the way for women in the profession during the last quarter of the twentieth century. The latter enlarged the scope of their expertise and secured acceptance.

Stamina and perseverance in the face of disapprobation characterize the predecessors of the twenty-first century women attorneys. An awareness of this history should serve as motivation to play an even larger role in their profession, in government, and in the justice system.

Sara B. Rearden, 1971.

M. Corinne Blanks, 1972.

M. Carrington Salley, 1972.

Treva G. Ashworth, 1973.

Darra Williamson Cothran, 1973.

Mary Elizabeth Crum, 1973.

Sandra M. Schraibman, 1973.

Ann M. Stirling, 1974.

Victoria L. Eslinger, 1974.

Dorothy A. Manigault, 1974.

Adele J. Pope, 1974.

*Chief Justice Jean Hoefer Toal of the South Carolina Supreme Court,
March 23, 2000.*

Bibliography

Bernard, Jessie. *The Female World,* The Free Press, a division of MacMillan Publishing Co., Inc., 1981.

Cote, Richard. *Mary's World,* Corinthian Books, Mt. Pleasant, 2001.

Cushman, Claire, Editor. *Supreme Court Decisions and Women's Rights,* Foreword by Associate Justice Ruth Bader Ginsburg, CQ Press, a division of the Congressional Quarterly, Inc., 2001.

Edgar, Walter. *South Carolina: A History,* University of South Carolina Press, 1998.

Farrow, Tiera. *Lawyer in Petticoats,* Vantage Press, Inc., New York, 1953.

Garza, Hedda. *Barred from the Bar: A History of Women and the Legal Profession,* Franklin Watts, a division of Grober Publishing, New York, 1996.

Goldberg, David J. *Discontented America: The United States in the 1920s,* The Johns Hopkins University Press, Baltimore, 1999.

Harragan, Betty Lehan. *Games Mother Never Taught You: Corporate Gamesmanship for Women,* Rawson Associates Publishers, Inc., New York, 1977.

Kanter, Rosabeth Moss. *Men and Women of the Corporation,* Basic Books, a member of The Books Group, 1977.

McCandless, Amy Thompson. *The Past in the Present: Women's Higher Education in Twentieth-Century American South,* The University of Alabama Press, Tuscaloosa and London, 1999.

Menand, Louis. "The Seventies Show," *The New Yorker,* May 28, 2001.

Morello, Karen Berger. *The Invisible Bar: The Woman Lawyer in America, 1638 to the Present,* Random House, New York, 1986.

Ophycke, Sandra. "Women in America," *The Routeledge Historical Atlas,* Routledge, New York and London, 2000.

Rogers, George C. *Generations of Lawyers: A History of the South Carolina Bar,* The South Carolina Bar Foundation, 1992.

Rosen, Robert. *A Short History of Charleston,* Lexikos, San Francisco, 1992.

Someone, Angela. *Academic Women Working towards Equality,* Bergin & Garvey Publishers, Inc., Massachusetts, 1987.

Wallace, David Duncan. *South Carolina: A Short History*, University of South Carolina Press, 1961.

Ware, Susan. *Modern American Women: A Documentary History,* The McGraw-Hill Companies, 1997.

$\mathcal{I}ndex$

-A-

-C-

Nichols and Wyche
(Spartanburg) 21
Nineteenth Amendment 25, 26
SC ratifies 140
Nixon, Richard M. 77
Norfolk Southern Railway 54
Norris, Ella Rebecca 2
North Carolina A&T
University 169
North Carolina Central
University Law School 147

-O-

O'Bryan, William M. 35
O'Connor, Sandra Day 179
"O'Connor v. United States,"
No. 85-158, 55 U.S.LW.
4007 (11-4-86) 129
O'Malveny and Myers 188
"Only Six Million Acres" 189
opening prayers in court. *See*
invocations
"Opera in Greenville" 85–86,
93-94
Orangeburg High School 89
"Orangeburg Times and
Democrat" 29
Order of the Coif 153
Ott, Milldege T. 94
Our Lady of Mercy Catholic
Church (Charleston, SC) 53
Owens, Elsie Haynsworth
Taylor 92

-P-

Padgett and Moore
(Walterboro, SC) 88
Padgett, James G. 88
Palmetto Legal Services 174,
175
Parler, Ed 97
Paschal, Gary 153
Paschal, Kay Frances 152–153,
161
Patton, George C. 116
Pearl Harbor 67
Pearlman, Gus H. 46
Pearson, Patricia. *See* Brehmer,
Patricia O'Dell
Peeples, Isaac S., Jr. 75
Perry, James Margrave (Miss
Jim) 14, 15-17, 23, 112, 128
Perry, James Margrave, Mr. 16
Perry, Jeanne LeGal 16
Perry, Matthew J. 124
Phi Beta Kappa 31, 128, 153,
185
Piedmont Legal Services, Inc.
See Spartanburg Legal Aid
Society
Pierce, Tressie Jean 29-30, 31
Planned Parenthood League
136
"Playboy" 103
Poe, Hazel Collings. *See*
Collings, Hazel Cover
Polatty, Nancy Elizabeth 158